GUIDELINES

VOL 32 / PART 2
May–August 2016

Commissioned by **David Spriggs**; *Edited by* **Lisa Cherrett**

GW00691705

Guidelines © BRF 2016

The Bible Reading Fellowship
15 The Chambers, Vineyard, Abingdon OX14 3FE
Tel: 01865 319700; Fax: 01865 319701
E-mail: enquiries@brf.org.uk; Websites: www.brf.org.uk; www.biblereadingnotes.org.uk

ISBN 978 0 85746 393 7

Distributed in Australia by Mediacom Education Inc., PO Box 610, Unley, SA 5061.
Tel: 1800 811 311; Fax: 08 8297 8719;
E-mail: admin@mediacom.org.au
Available also from all good Christian bookshops in Australia.
For individual and group subscriptions in Australia:
Mrs Rosemary Morrall, PO Box W35, Wanniassa, ACT 2903.

Distributed in New Zealand by Scripture Union Wholesale, PO Box 760, Wellington
Tel: 04 385 0421; Fax: 04 384 3990; E-mail: suwholesale@clear.net.nz

Publications distributed to more than 60 countries

Acknowledgments

The New Revised Standard Version of the Bible, Anglicised Edition, copyright © 1989, 1995 by the Division of Christian Education of the National Council of the Churches of Christ in the USA. Used by permission. All rights reserved.

The Holy Bible, New International Version (Anglicised Edition), copyright © 1979, 1984, 2011 by Biblica. Used by permission of Hodder & Stoughton Publishers, an Hachette UK company. All rights reserved. 'NIV' is a registered trademark of Biblica. UK trademark number 1448790.

The New American Standard Bible®, Copyright © 1960, 1962, 1963, 1968, 1971, 1972, 1973, 1975, 1977, 1995 by The Lockman Foundation. Used by permission. (www.Lockman.org)

Printed by Gutenberg Press, Tarxien, Malta.

Suggestions for using *Guidelines*

Set aside a regular time and place, if possible, when you can read and pray undisturbed. Before you begin, take time to be still and, if you find it helpful, use the BRF prayer.

In *Guidelines*, the introductory section provides context for the passages or themes to be studied, while the units of comment can be used daily, weekly, or whatever best fits your timetable. You will need a Bible (more than one if you want to compare different translations) as Bible passages are not included. At the end of each week is a 'Guidelines' section, offering further thoughts about, or practical application of what you have been studying.

Occasionally, you may read something in *Guidelines* that you find particularly challenging, even uncomfortable. This is inevitable in a series of notes which draws on a wide spectrum of contributors, and doesn't believe in ducking difficult issues. Indeed, we believe that *Guidelines* readers much prefer thought-provoking material to a bland diet that only confirms what they already think.

If you do disagree with a contributor, you may find it helpful to go through these three steps. First, think about why you feel uncomfortable. Perhaps this is an idea that is new to you, or you are not happy at the way something has been expressed. Or there may be something more substantial—you may feel that the writer is guilty of sweeping generalisation, factual error, theological or ethical misjudgment. Second, pray that God would use this disagreement to teach you more about his word and about yourself. Third, think about what you will do as a result of the disagreement. You might resolve to find out more about the issue, or write to the contributor or the editors of *Guidelines*.

To send feedback, you may email or write to BRF at the addresses shown opposite. If you would like your comment to be included on our website, please email connect@brf.org.uk. You can also Tweet to @brfonline, using the hashtag #brfconnect.

Writers in this issue

Jeremy Duff is Team Vicar in South Widnes. His teaching and writing ministry has included posts at Liverpool Cathedral and Oxford University. His book *The Elements of New Testament Greek* (2005) is Cambridge University Press's bestselling religion title.

Brian Howell has lectured in Old Testament at several universities and institutions around the UK, and is currently the Dean of Studies and Research at Bible Society. He is also a jazz saxophonist and professional kid wrestler (but only against the fearsome tag team of Jayden and Jazmine).

David Spriggs has retired from Bible Society but continues his work with them as a consultant. His main role is as a team minister at the Hinckley Baptist Church, with special responsibility to work with the leaders.

Hugh Williamson was the Regius Professor of Hebrew at Oxford University until he retired in 2014. He has written extensively on the books of Chronicles, Ezra and Nehemiah, and on Isaiah. He preaches regularly in his home church in Southwold, Suffolk.

Maggie Guite is an Anglican priest. During the 1980s she taught Doctrine in two colleges of the Cambridge Theological Federation. Since then she has been serving in various parishes in the Diocese of Ely and is currently parish priest of St Mark's, Cambridge, and an honorary canon of Ely.

Ian Paul is Associate Minister at St Nic's Nottingham, and Honorary Assistant Professor at the University of Nottingham, as well as Managing Editor at Grove Books in Cambridge. He blogs at www.Psephizo.com.

Derek Tidball is a Baptist minister, author and speaker, who was principal of London School of Theology and is currently visiting scholar at Spurgeon's College, London.

P.W. (Bill) Goodman encourages and enables life-long learning among fellow clergy in the Anglican Diocese of Lincoln, as Continuing Ministerial Development Officer. He has been part of ministry training courses in the UK and overseas, and currently teaches at the Lincoln School of Theology.

Andrew Rogers is Principal Lecturer in Practical Theology at the University of Roehampton, where he runs an ecumenical degree programme for students engaged in Christian ministry. Andrew is the author of *Congregational Hermeneutics: How do we read?* (Ashgate, 2015).

David Spriggs writes...

Pentecost is a profoundly important festival for the Christian church. The Holy Spirit provides us with the theological and experiential bridge between the Jesus of the Gospels and the Christ of our faith today. Pentecost is about the authenticity of and authorisation for the mission of the church, and God's promise that his transforming presence is at work within us. Pentecost is not only a Christian festival day; it is the Christian context for life today.

The most clearly 'Pentecostal' material in this issue is by Jeremy Duff, as he takes us through John's insights on the Holy Spirit in Jesus' teaching. Luke 5—9, our lectionary Gospel material, illustrates the outworking of Jesus' Spirit-anointed life in all his personal encounters.

Brian Howell leads us through 1 Kings, where God's people seek to work out how to play their part among the world powers. We discover the challenge of Elijah to God's people to return fully to their God, as well as the struggles of the divided nations of Judah and Israel to cope with military pressures.

Ezra and Nehemiah, explained by Derek Tidball and Bill Goodman respectively, further illuminate the resources of God and the complexities of living for him in constantly changing environments. Each in their own way can stimulate us as we try to work out what authentic Christian living looks like in our changing landscapes.

Included in this issue is the first instalment of Hugh Williamson's rich insights about the early chapters of Isaiah, in which there are some remarkable passages about God's Spirit. Then Maggie Guite opens up the rather difficult book of Zechariah. Of special interest is the way in which she associates the later chapters with Gospel sayings.

Part of the challenge of Zechariah is that it includes proto-apocalyptic literature. A more developed form, Revelation 4—22, is expertly unwrapped for us by Ian Paul. The Spirit-anointed people of God face many struggles, immersed in a hostile world, but they contribute to the unfolding purpose of God to renew the whole creation.

The final contribution is from a new writer for us, Andrew Rogers. He tackles Galatians, a book that shows Paul's fury and his sensitivities to the gospel, as well as providing the gem about the transforming impact of the fruit of the Spirit.

Throughout this edition are the twin themes of the role of God's Spirit in the life of his community and the challenge to live authentically in difficult and changing environments.

The Holy Spirit in John's Gospel

The early church told stories of how John's Gospel was written after the other three, as a different sort—a spiritual one, an eagle soaring high above the other 'earthbound' Gospels. Matthew, Mark and Luke do form a group, different from John (even if some scholars believe that John was actually written before Luke, and hence that John was one of the 'predecessors' mentioned by Luke in 1:1–4). John's Gospel is full of discussion and theological reflection, as key ideas are chewed over time and time again from differing perspectives. Key words, such as 'sent', 'light' and 'love', are woven throughout the Gospel.

We see this played out in John's discussion of the Holy Spirit. Some of the key references from the other Gospels are there—the Spirit descending on Jesus at his baptism, the promise that Jesus will baptise with the Spirit, the observation that God's Spirit is at work in Jesus, and the need to wait for the Spirit who will come after Jesus. However, in John we find these ideas explored more deeply.

Three times 'spirit' is used in relation to Jesus in a 'human sense' (for example, 11:33: 'he was deeply moved in spirit'; see also 13:21; 19:30). Otherwise, we find 'the Spirit' mentioned twelve times in John's Gospel. Half of these occurrences are spread across the first 13 chapters; there is then a far more concentrated discussion of the Spirit in chapters 14—16 (five references), and a final reference in chapter 20. Over the next two weeks we will examine each of these references to build up an overall sense of the Spirit in John's Gospel.

NB: Throughout these notes I have referred to the Spirit as 'he'. The Spirit is a person, not a thing (so cannot be described as 'it') but is without gender. There is no satisfactory way around this issue in modern English. Genesis 1:27 perhaps implies that God is male *and* female: there is certainly no reason for preferring either 'he' or 'she' for the Spirit.

Quotations are taken from the New International Version unless otherwise indicated.

1 Baptised by the Spirit

John 1:19–34

Who speaks for God? Who represents him or acts on his behalf? It's a troubling question. God's work is often done through people, but we tend to shy away from people who claim that they have a 'hotline' to God.

This is where we start our journey in John's Gospel. John the Baptist has drawn people's attention because his actions seem significant. 'Christ', 'Elijah' and 'the Prophet' (a prophet like Moses, see Deuteronomy 18:18) are all figures who might be seen as bringing in or marking God's return to his people, and John applies to himself (v. 23) the words of Isaiah 40:3, which speak of people in the desert preparing for God to come to them. John agrees that this is the moment when God is coming close to his people, and the key figure is here—but it's not him. So who is it? How do we tell who speaks for God?

John's answer is clear: the one who has God's Spirit is the one who represents God. John has seen God's Spirit descend on Jesus. He is the one. Jesus' role is described in different terms: he is the one who will deal with sin (v. 29), the supreme one (v. 30) and the one who will baptise with the Spirit (v. 33). In the language of the religious authorities, Jesus is the Messiah, Elijah and the Prophet. The details of these different names are not the point. What matters is that Jesus is the one representing God, who will bring about a meeting with God, and he is marked out for that task by God's own Spirit. There are no qualities, training programmes or skills that can make someone fit to represent God. It is only God's Spirit in Jesus that makes him fit to represent God, fit to be God's Son, fit to be the one who reconnects God with his people.

There is one more thing. Jesus is also going to baptise others with the Spirit. Then, presumably, they will share his work of representing God in the world, bringing people back to him. Who speaks for God? Who represents God? The one filled with God's Spirit—that is, Jesus and those he baptises. We should not be surprised, for 'God is spirit' (John 4:24). God's action in our world is always a matter of Spirit.

2 Born of Spirit

Nicodemus is halfway there. He has realised that Jesus is 'from God' and that God is with him. Jesus' miracles have persuaded him of this: he has seen them as miraculous 'signs' (v. 2), pointing to the fact that God is with Jesus. What really matters is God's presence (through his Spirit).

Jesus does not leave it there, however. What about Nicodemus himself? What about us? How are we going to be part of God's people and plan (the phrases 'see God's kingdom' in verse 3 and 'enter God's kingdom' in verse 5 seem to mean the same thing). Is it sufficient for us to have the Spirit-filled Jesus as our leader?

No, we must be 'born again'. The Greek word translated as 'again' could also mean 'from above', and both meanings seem to be in view. Jesus is talking about a 'second birth', but it is not just a repeat of our first birth. It is a birth 'of the Spirit' rather than of the flesh, and 'from above'. ('Water and the Spirit' in verse 5 puzzles commentators, but is probably a reference to baptism being both 'of water' and 'of Spirit'.)

What does this mean? Being 'born again' is a very powerful image of a complete transformation—not just a 'fresh start' but an emergence into a completely different world. Being born again means becoming a child again, just starting out, having to learn. It means leaving behind all that we have accumulated, whether skills or possessions. And someone who has been born again is fundamentally dislocated from our world, even alien to it. They will be like the wind, present in our world but something that we cannot understand or pin down (v. 8). Indeed, since the Greek word for 'wind' is the same as 'spirit', those who are born of the Spirit take on this quality of the Spirit itself. It is not that they become erratic and unpredictable, but that they live in a fundamentally different way, which 'makes no sense'. People see the effects of our lives but do not understand the logic or purpose.

It isn't sufficient for Nicodemus to recognise and follow the one who has God's Spirit with him. He also needs to undergo a radical transformation, so that he too becomes 'of Spirit'. The same is true for us.

3 Spirit without limit

The two previous passages have emphasised that Jesus' followers must share in being baptised 'by the Spirit' or 'of the Spirit'. We are not called to remain as we were, while following a new spiritual teacher. We are called to be transformed by the Spirit ourselves. However, this does not mean that we become just like Jesus. We might be 'Spirit people', as Jesus is, but the difference between us is not just a matter of degree; it's not just that he has 'a bit more' Spirit than we do.

John the Baptist demonstrates this important point. John was great (see Jesus' praise of him in Luke 7:28). He was the one 'sent ahead' (v. 28); he is the 'best man' at the wedding (v. 29). But he is to become less, while Jesus becomes greater.

What makes this fundamental difference? God. For 'a person can receive only what is given them from heaven' (v. 27). Jesus is 'from above', 'from heaven'. He can speak of what he has seen in heaven (v. 32). Compare John 1:18: 'No one has ever seen God. It is God the only Son, who is close to the Father's heart, who has made him known' (NRSV). What we receive is dependent on him. We may indeed have the Spirit, but Jesus has it 'without limit' (v. 34). Everything has been given to him. Therefore he is the decisive factor in judgement: eternal life is dependent on our response to him.

Paul describes Jesus as being 'the image' of God (Colossians 1:15), whereas humanity is made 'in the image of God' (Genesis 1:27). Humanity's position ('in the image') is both similar to and fundamentally distinct from Jesus' position ('the image'). Similarly, Jesus receives the Spirit from God, while we receive the Spirit only as Jesus gives it to us (see John 20:21–22). We receive the Spirit, but Jesus alone receives it 'without limit'.

Limits are a fundamental aspect of human lives. How do you cope with them? What limits are you coming up against? How might it be relevant for you that Jesus, unlike us, receives from God 'without limit' and can therefore fully reveal and represent God? Indeed, is there something to learn from John's words, that we might need to become less so that Jesus can become greater?

2–8 May   9

4 Worship in Spirit

The Samaritan woman is asking Jesus about one of the fundamental disagreements between the Samaritans and the Jews. Should God be worshipped on Mount Gerizim (in Samaria) or in the Jerusalem temple (in Judea)? (She doesn't seem to be asking the Jews to worship on Gerizim; she simply wants them to recognise the legitimacy of Gerizim as a place for the Samaritans to worship.)

Jesus' reply highlights two important points. First, all is changing: 'a time is coming and has now come' (v. 23). There has been a certain priority for the Jewish people (v. 22), but this distinction is coming to an end. In the new era, neither Gerizim nor Jerusalem is important. This is similar to Paul's argument in Romans 1:16 that the gospel 'is the power of God that brings salvation to everyone who believes: first to the Jew, then to the Gentile'. It is for everyone without exception, but it came 'first' to the Jews (see also Romans 2:9–11).

These arguments about Judaism may seem slightly obscure, but the idea that the people who have been around longest are the most important is deeply rooted in our churches. Great annoyance can be caused if the newcomer's opinion is taken just as seriously as the opinion of someone who has been a leading light for 40 years!

Second, Jesus is pointing to a change in the nature of worship, away from earthly practicalities like location (or, we might say, arguments over musical style or the use of written liturgy and objects such as icons or candles). In the new era, worship needs to be 'in spirit and truth'. It is a mistake to try to wring out from this phrase some ammunition to use in battles over worship styles, since anyone can claim that their preferred style is 'in spirit'. The point is that worship is about God, who is fundamentally different from us. It is outside our normal ways of operating. In the language of the previous passages, it is 'of spirit', not 'of flesh'.

It's easy for worship to become about other things—musical excellence, warmth and welcome, bringing people together, expressing a continuity or discontinuity with tradition—but it should be about God. Therefore, connecting with God's Spirit must take precedence over all other worthy considerations that are simply 'of flesh'.

5 The Spirit gives life

John 6:51–65

Jesus has just been comparing his feeding of the 5000 with the feeding of the Israelites with manna in the desert. But he doesn't just claim that his bread is better, or even that his bread is life-giving and truly 'from heaven' (manna being merely 'heaven-sent'). He claims that *he* is the living bread and that people need to eat his flesh and drink his blood (vv. 51–54). This is a truly shocking statement, and it is not surprising that it caused not just public argument but grumbling among Jesus' own disciples (vv. 52, 61)

For us (and presumably for the Gospel writer), Jesus' words about bread, flesh and blood remind us of Holy Communion. But John is not simply referring to Communion in an obscure fashion. Throughout this dialogue—and, indeed, throughout the gospel—physical things are used to speak of spiritual realities. We see this in John 6:27, when Jesus says, 'Do not work for food that spoils, but for food that endures to eternal life, which the Son of Man will give you.' Here Jesus is seeking to point the people away from literal bread, which sustains this life, to spiritual food, which sustains eternal life. In the language of 6:35, Jesus is the 'bread of life' in as much as 'whoever comes to me will never go hungry' (that is, they will be spiritually sustained). He is true food (v. 55), of which what we would call physical food is only a shadow.

What matters is the connection between us and Jesus—we being in him and he being in us (v. 56: compare John 15:1–10, words spoken at the point when, in Mark, Matthew and Luke, Jesus shares the last supper). This is why, at the end of the passage, Jesus can easily move on from the language of bread, flesh and blood to say, 'The Spirit gives life' (v. 63). In the end, it is only the life-giving Spirit, coming down from heaven, who can truly sustain (as we saw on days 2 and 3 this week). Earthly activities—including Communion and worship (see day 4)—have their purpose only in as much as they point us to and draw us into a relationship with God 'in spirit'.

6 The Spirit flowing

John 7:37–39

The Festival of Tabernacles (7:2) was one of the three great pilgrim festivals (Deuteronomy 16:16) that brought many people to Jerusalem. It celebrated God's provision for his people, both in that year's harvest and during the 40 years in the desert during the exodus. On the last and greatest day (v. 37), there was a 'water ceremony' in which water was poured out in the temple as a symbol of God's overflowing provision. Thus, Jesus' words about thirst and living water have particular significance here: imagine someone declaring on Christmas Day that 'God's Word' is in them, or announcing on Easter Day that they can conquer death.

There are three steps in this passage. First, Jesus claims to be the source of true thirst-quenching water. The context gives it additional power: Jesus is effectively claiming that God's provision for his people is now found in him, not in these temple rituals. Psalm 107 and Isaiah 35 describe how God himself provides water for his thirsty people: that provision is now made by Jesus.

Second, John explicitly links this provision to the Spirit who will be given after Jesus' resurrection (v. 39). In John 6:51–65, we saw that beneath all the discussion of bread, life, flesh and blood was an understanding that it is really the Spirit who gives life. These other things are just ways of thinking about, or connecting with, God's presence in Jesus and, hence, God's Spirit. Here in John 7 we see that 'coming to Jesus' (v. 37) and 'believing in Jesus' (v. 38) have their power because they lead to the gift of the Spirit. It's an important reminder that our connection to God is, in the end, God's work, dependent on God's Spirit.

Third, Jesus says that the living water, the Spirit, will flow out from within them (v. 38). Perhaps this just means that it will be 'overflowing', 'more than enough', like the water poured down the temple steps. It may also point to God's gift flowing out to the benefit of others. We need to be careful. 'Baptising in Spirit' is an activity of Jesus alone; God sends the Spirit in *Jesus'* name (14:26). The 'spring' is established in us only by Jesus; we cannot provide God's Spirit to others, yet perhaps its benefits flow from us and refresh others.

Guidelines

Spiritual but not religious? It's odd that the words 'spirituality' and 'Christianity' (even more so, 'spirituality' and 'church') are not connected to each other in most people's minds. For many, the church is connected with ideas of community, dependability, tradition, morality, care and good deeds, but it is not a place where someone would go to explore 'spirituality'.

Our readings this week challenge that disconnection. It has been made clear in different ways that, in the end, being a Christian is all about 'the Spirit'. The Spirit comes to us from Jesus, and his benefits may flow out from us to others. Physical things and religious rituals may point to the Spirit, but what matters in the end is the Spirit. Being a Christian is all about being Spirit-ual.

You probably think that anyway, but would you adopt the phrase 'spiritual, not religious' for yourself? What difference would it make if you did? How would you be changed if you saw yourself—each day, each hour, at home and at work—as someone filled to overflowing with God's Spirit?

1 Spirit like Jesus

John 14:8–20

Five of our six readings this week come from the 'farewell discourses'—Jesus' discussions with his disciples on the night before he died. They pick up the thread from our last passage: the Spirit has not yet been given, but will be soon. What will he be like?

The focus of this first passage is on seeing 'the Father'. Jesus appears frustrated with Philip's lack of comprehension (v. 9), as we see elsewhere in the Gospels (for example, Mark 4:40), but we might have sympathy with Philip's request. It is one thing to think that Jesus will reveal God (1:18, 3:13), but he is asking for something more. Jesus claims that he is not just communicating the Father, but in some sense embodies the Father: 'anyone who has seen me has seen the Father' (v. 9).

In the opening verses of his Gospel, John presented the same idea by talking about 'the Word', which 'was God' (1:1), 'became flesh' (v. 14) and was seen as Jesus (vv. 14–18). Paul uses the language of 'image', describing Jesus as 'the image of the invisible God' (Colossians 1:15), while Hebrews 1:3 calls him 'the exact imprint of God's very being' (NRSV).

The idea that Jesus is going away, to his Father, permeates the whole passage (14:2–3, 12, 18–19). In this context, Jesus states that he will ask the Father to send 'another advocate'. Thus he will, in effect, come back to them (vv. 16–18). Grammatically, 'another' here means 'another of the same kind' (as in 'pass me another apple'). 'Advocate' means someone who comes alongside to help you and plead your case. Other translations use the word 'counsellor', which means someone you trust to give you wise advice, not someone who listens to problems.

Thus we see that the Spirit is a sort of replacement Jesus who will continue Jesus' presence among them and his support of them, so that they truly are not left as 'orphans' (v. 18). This Spirit will be in them (v. 17), and Jesus himself is in them, and they are in him (v. 20). It's hard for us not to think that it would be better if we saw Jesus 'in the flesh', but Jesus says that the opposite is true (vv. 12, 18–20). Do we need a greater, but also more intimate, view of the Spirit as Jesus alongside us?

2 The Spirit, the teacher

John 14:21–31

The Spirit, as we have seen, is to be 'a replacement Jesus', but what does this mean? Some things are clear. He is not 'God made flesh', as Jesus was. Yet he does bring Jesus' presence to them so strongly that they are 'in him' and he is 'in them'(14:20).

Verse 26 is crucial for exploring the relationship between Jesus and the Spirit. The Spirit is sent 'in Jesus' name', which emphasises that the disciples' receipt of the Spirit is dependent on Jesus. The Spirit is not a separate manifestation of God, as if some people could come to God through the Spirit, and others through Jesus. He is not a 'second Jesus' in the sense of a second revelation of God: he continues Jesus' work. We see this expressed in a different way in the first verse of the book of Acts, which reads, 'In my former book [Luke's Gospel], Theophilus, I wrote about all that Jesus began to do and to teach until the day he was taken up to heaven'. This implies that Acts will show what Jesus *continued* 'to do and to teach', despite the fact that Jesus is physically absent from Acts. He continues to do and teach through the Spirit.

The Spirit will 'will teach you all things' and 'will remind you of everything I have said to you' (v. 26). I think it is right to take these phrases together. The Spirit will teach them everything they need. Jesus has actually already told them 'everything' (15:15), but they will need 'reminding' of it. At the time, of course, they misunderstood or resisted much of what Jesus said, so 'reminding' is a euphemism here. But the point is that the Spirit will not add anything, but will only help them remember and understand what Jesus himself taught. Indeed, this is the key to understanding the difference between John on the one hand and Mark, Matthew and Luke on the other. The other Gospels tell us what the disciples understood (or misunderstood) at the time. John tells us what they understood of Jesus' meaning afterwards, with the Spirit's help.

This passage, like others, such as Matthew 28:16–20 (the great commission), emphasises our need to obey Jesus' teaching. Now, though, we see that we can only remember, understand and have a chance of following that teaching through the work of God's Spirit.

3 Testifying Spirit

John 15:18–27

These are challenging words. Verses 18 and 19 do not strictly imply, 'If the world loves you, you belong to the world and you are not my disciples'; however, they come pretty close to it. Verse 20 does seem to say that if we are truly Jesus' disciples, we will be persecuted. Are you? Many of our sisters and brothers across the world are persecuted, but are you? Of course, there is no virtue in deliberately being obnoxious and rude about faith, just so that people won't like us, and one might see the 'hate'/'love' contrast as being starkly drawn for effect. But it is challenging to realise that Jesus expects us as his followers to experience a dislocation and, at times, at least a tension with the world around us.

The description of the Spirit's role here is new. So far in our study, the Spirit has always been seen as acting in relation to Jesus' followers, giving life, refreshment, comfort and teaching. Here, however, he testifies about Jesus to the world ('them' in verses 22 and 24). It can't mean that he testifies or confirms the truth to us, because we too are told to testify (v. 27). This work is, though, the work of a 'replacement Jesus', for the Spirit is testifying to Jesus (v. 26), not simply to God. In doing so, he is continuing Jesus' work of speaking and showing the truth to the people.

What difference does it make to realise that the Spirit testifies to Jesus directly, not just by teaching and empowering us? It both challenges and comforts me to recognise that God's work is not dependent on me. God's Spirit is already out there in the world; God's mission goes forward without me! Indeed, my role is (as so many people have said) to 'see what God is doing and join in'. This is a challenge to my pride and sense of self-importance, but it is also a comfort: God's work does not all depend on me. We are called to join with God's Spirit (v. 27). We are important, but God is not limited by us.

4 Convicting Spirit

John 16:5–12

This passage picks up some of the earlier ideas about the Spirit and brings them together. In John 14:4–9, Thomas and Philip asked about Jesus' departure; as the conversation continued, Jesus' explanation began to take a negative tone, with warnings that the world would hate them (15:18–19), reject them and even kill them (16:2). As all this starts to sink in, it is unsurprising that the disciples are filled with grief. It really does seem as if Jesus is abandoning them to a terrible fate.

Once again Jesus emphasises that they (and therefore we) are better off without him. We are better off with the replacement, with the Spirit. Presumably this is not because the Spirit is better in general. Rather, Jesus came to do a particular task, which he will soon declare to be finished (19:30). For the next task—empowering a growing, worldwide community—the Spirit will be better. How hard it is, sometimes, to recognise that a new development can be better for the future without implying that there was a problem in the past. We may have done a great job, but it can still be best if we stop. Some activity or approach may have borne much fruit so far, and still not be right for the future.

Earlier (15:22–27) we read that 'the world' is guilty because it has ignored Jesus' words and miracles, and that the Spirit will testify to Jesus. Again we see the Spirit continuing Jesus' work, for now it is the Spirit who convicts the world of its guilt in relation to Jesus. The triplet of sin, righteousness and judgement (v. 8) unpacks aspects of this 'guilt'. The wrong that is being done ('sin') is not believing in Jesus: this is the fundamental choice that people face. The fact that Jesus was indeed speaking for God, that his claims were right ('righteousness'), will be demonstrated by his departure to the Father (just as the resurrection proved that God was with Jesus: Mark 14:61–62). The fact that 'judgement' will come is demonstrated by God's decisive actions against 'the ruler of this world' (Luke 10:17–20; John 12:31–33). All of this is the Spirit's work because he is the one who continues to 'remind' us of all these truths. Is it important to know that 'convicting others of guilt' is the Spirit's work, not ours?

5 Revealing Spirit

John 16:13–15

This final description of the work of the Spirit underlines some key points. The Spirit is reliable: he is 'of truth', he guides 'into all the truth', and he speaks 'only what he hears [from the Father]' (v. 13). This reliability is important because his function is to reveal the truth to the disciples. Earlier (14:26) we saw that he will both 'teach you all things' and 'remind you of everything I have said'. Here again we find that all knowledge and truth belongs to Jesus (v. 15) and he has shared it all with his disciples (15:15); therefore, teaching all things is the same as 'reminding' them of what Jesus has said (making clear what Jesus meant, even though they didn't grasp it at the time). At the same time, this passage re-emphasises the Spirit as 'a replacement Jesus'. He does not provide a new, independent revelation of God; he points back to and is, in a sense, dependent on Jesus—communicating between Jesus and his followers (vv. 14–15).

There is something new, though. The Spirit will 'tell you what is yet to come' (v. 13). Throughout history, there have been those who have focused on the Spirit's role in illuminating the scriptures, and those who have seen him at work in prophecy, including prophecy about the future.

In the church, this is often described as a battle between 'institutional' elements (wanting to keep the Spirit in a box, merely helping us understand Jesus better) and 'charismatic' (wanting the Spirit to speak now, today, in powerful ways). These verses force us to be more balanced. They make abundantly clear that the Spirit does not 'go beyond' Jesus. He brings glory to Jesus and communicates only what he receives from Jesus. However, he does 'tell you what is yet to come'—giving insights, 'words of knowledge' and prophecy about the future.

This balance is reflected in the book of Revelation, which is clear that the 'prophecy' (1:3) has come from Jesus (v. 1) but has reached John through the action of the Spirit (v. 10). That prophecy does include 'what must soon take place' (v. 1), even if Revelation often seems to be revealing the truth about 'the way the world is' rather than only predicting events in the future.

Truth is powerful. As the Spirit leads us into truth, focused on Jesus, our present and the future are both changed and revealed.

6 Our Spirit

John 20:19–23

Finally, the long-promised Spirit is given. In Jesus, God came and 'lived among us' (1:14, NRSV); now, in the Spirit, God comes to live within us.

The Spirit comes in a context where fear is turned into joy and peace (vv. 19–20). It is Jesus' presence that has this effect. But if we have learnt anything in these two weeks, it is that the Spirit continues Jesus' work, and the Spirit will indeed bring joy and boldness to the growing church. It is interesting to ponder this 'prescription' of what we need—for fear to be replaced with joy and peace. The 'joy' element is noteworthy. People often say that faith in God brings peace, but are we known for joy?

The receipt of the Spirit is connected with 'sending' (v. 21). As Jesus was sent by the Father, so Jesus now sends us. The words 'as' and 'so' are important: we are sent in the same way as Jesus, to act in the same manner, and to continue his work. All the knowledge that the Father has given Jesus is now ours (15:15); Jesus and his followers are intimately connected (14:20). Those words also define our task: we are 'sent people'. Jesus found both acceptance and rejection in his work (1:10–13), and we should expect the same (15:20). It is valuable to ponder the idea that we are 'sent' people. Who do you feel 'sent' to?

The final verse about the forgiveness of sins is frightening. I would prefer not to have that power, for while I can trust God to be just, kind and merciful, I know that too often I am not. However, this forgiveness is part and parcel of being 'sent' as Jesus was sent. He was sent to bring salvation, yet in the process sin was revealed and judgement was an inevitable consequence for those who rejected him. So we too are sent to bring forgiveness and release to people, but the sad truth is that this can reinforce people in their rebellion against God.

We also have to recognise that the way we behave towards others can have a huge influence. Do we treat them as forgiven people, or do we remember the past and hold it against them? We can't duck the responsibility by arguing about whether we want this power or not. All we can do is try to use it as Jesus himself did.

Guidelines

This week's readings bring four challenges:

* Do we think of the Spirit as being 'Jesus with us', with the same compassion and love as Jesus himself has?
* Do we believe we are better off with the Spirit rather than Jesus, trusting that the Spirit 'reminds us' of everything that Jesus would teach us?
* Do we recognise that the Spirit is at work in the world, not just within us? Does that make a difference?
* Do we consciously receive and welcome God's Spirit?

1 Kings

1 Kings is not the tale of some minor monarchs in a small, remote ancient Near Eastern state. It is also not primarily concerned to chronicle the interactions of this vassal state with major empires and their sovereigns. Rather, it is the story of the great king who uses these rulers like servants to do his bidding. Unlike them, though, the just, patient and gracious character of this king resonates throughout the story of his people.

1 and 2 Kings were originally one book, though no author is mentioned for either part. 1 Kings covers a history spanning from Solomon's rise to power in 970BC to the death of King Ahab in 853BC (aligned with the battle of Qarqar, which resulted in a power shift equivalent in significance to the battle of Waterloo). This historical information has been coordinated with Assyrian and Babylonian records, which has convinced the vast majority of scholars of 1 Kings' impressive historical accuracy.

The book is generally considered to be written in the genre of 'prophetic narrative'. As Paul House explains, this genre includes five characteristics: '[assessing] the past based on God's covenant with Israel… predict[ing] the future by noting how God has blessed or punished Israel in the past and by noting what promises God has made… creat[ing] its plot by emphasising events that fulfil a prophetic view of the past and future… assess[ing] characters based on how they accelerate or retard the blessings or judgement… instruct[ing] its audience to turn to the Lord so they can receive blessing instead of punishment' (*1, 2 Kings*, Broadman & Holman, 1995, p. 58).

As Peter Leithart observes, the themes of law, wisdom, temple, prophets, and priesthood are all traced through the kings and brought to naught (*1&2 Kings*, Brazos, 2006, pp. 17–28). None of these symbols and institutions of the worship of God is able to effect a permanent change of heart. This message is being sent to those in exile to cause them to look toward the one thing that can—their true king.

Quotations are taken from the New American Standard Bible unless otherwise indicated.

1 Solomon's ascendency

1 Kings 1

The beginning of 1 Kings is often viewed by scholars as the conclusion of the 'succession narrative' begun in 2 Samuel 9. As it opens, we find the reign of King David at its finale, and it isn't a grand one. Since 2 Samuel 11—20, David has been on the receiving end of the action, most of which is a consequence of his sin, and now he appears defunct.

This initial episode of 1 Kings provides insight into the transition from David's reign to Solomon's, which is made difficult because Solomon's older brother Adonijah seeks to claim the throne. In a move that exposes both his audaciousness and foolishness, Adonijah proclaims himself king; previously, God chose the king through the prophet and confirmed him through his actions before the people.

Abishag is introduced in a passive role, much as Bathsheba was earlier. She underscores the frailty of a man so old that neither can blankets warm nor beauty arouse him. He does not 'know' her sexually (v. 4); nor, indeed, does he know much about what is happening in his kingdom (v. 18). In fact, there is a pun on the word 'king' (*melek*), when David responds to the accusation that he doesn't know what's going on in his kingdom with 'What to you?' (*mah-lka*) (v. 16).

In stark contrast with Abishag is Bathsheba. She was seen as a pawn when David committed adultery with her (2 Samuel 11) but here she is very much the protagonist. A clue to the change lies in the titles given to her at these different times. Whereas in 2 Samuel she is described as the 'wife of Uriah', here she is called the 'mother of Solomon'. She hasn't changed, but the emphasis in the story has: she is now involved because of her relationship to her son, not her husband. To this extent, she is now seen as a fully active character. Her name means 'daughter of oath', and, with Nathan's help, she reminds David of his promise to make her son king.

2 Death and consolidation

David counsels Solomon before his death, and what he says has often struck commentators as harsh and out of character for God's favoured king. However, part of the author's approach is to paint a full picture of the king, including the honourable and despicable qualities. David's advice is twofold: obey the Lord and secure the kingdom. The latter depends upon the former, as it is in obeying God's laws that Solomon can gain success in his ventures as well as maintaining God's favour towards his father's line.

In terms of securing the kingdom, David advises Solomon on dealing with several tricky characters. Joab, the maverick commander of David's army, is the greatest threat to Solomon's throne and is the only person, beside the prophet Nathan and Bathsheba herself, who knows of David's adultery and the subsequent murder of Uriah. In advising Solomon to have Joab killed, David may also be stating his own innocence in the deaths of Israelite commanders Amasa and Abner, whom Joab slew of his own accord (vv. 4–5; 2 Samuel 3:27; 20:10). Executing Joab would prevent their families from entertaining any thoughts of blood vengeance against David's son. It is curious that David did not feel capable of carrying out this execution himself, at an earlier date, but Joab's siding with Adonijah (1 Kings 1:19) gives him the opportunity to act.

The bright spot in David's advice is the mention of his friendship with the family of Barzillai, who was loyal to David (v. 7). This loyalty contrasts sharply with the behaviour of Shimei, who cursed David, perhaps making some claim to power on behalf of King Saul's tribe, Benjamin.

Some questions have been raised about Bathsheba's awareness of Adonijah's political machinations. When he asks her to go to Solomon on his behalf to ask for Abishag as a wife (v. 17), he is clearly making a power play. One act of a conqueror is to despoil the kingdom's harem, thus demonstrating the usurper's power and the impotence of the former ruler (see 2 Samuel 16:21). However, Bathsheba seems to be very much aware of this when she repeats Adonijah's words nearly verbatim—nearly. She adds 'your brother' (v. 21). This addition could be meant to distinguish him from all the other Adonijahs in the kingdom, but it is more likely that she is emphasising his threat to Solomon's rule. Only a brother would have a claim to the throne, making this act one of treason.

3 Solomon's prayer for wisdom

1 Kings 3:1–15

Solomon's marriage to an Egyptian princess, as soon as his reign is established, demonstrates that Israel is rising in the estimation of its neighbours as a power worthy of such an alliance, as marriage was used to seal peace accords. However, it also gives prior warning of his Achilles' heel—women. He will become famous for the size of his harem, which will eventually turn his heart from serving the Lord fully, and towards other gods (11:4).

The building of the temple, palace and walls marks a centralisation that has political and religious ramifications. Worship is currently offered on the high places—something of which God clearly disapproves, as it is mentioned as the only exception to Solomon's love for God and his following in his father's footsteps (v. 3). Although the people are said to worship there only because the temple has not yet been built, for Solomon, living in Jerusalem, the use of high places anticipates his downfall.

Solomon's request, literally for a 'hearing heart' (v. 9), brings echoes of Eden. Like Eve and Adam, Solomon seeks wisdom, to 'discern between good and evil'. However, whereas the primeval couple sought to 'know' good and evil apart from God (having moral autonomy, determining good and evil for themselves), Solomon seeks this knowledge *from* God.

Despite God's offer in verse 5, 'Ask for *whatever* you want me to give you', there is some small print. God responds to Solomon's humble request: 'Since you have asked… I will do what you have asked' (vv. 11–12). This would imply that the long life God promises is conditional upon Solomon's, and his successors', obedience (compare 2 Kings 20:3–6). This sort of implied condition is repeated in all of God's direct speech to Solomon (see 1 Kings 6:11–13; 9:3–9; 11:11–13) and, later, becomes the grounds to demonstrate the failure of the Israelite kings in this arrangement.

Nevertheless, Solomon had no equal 'in his lifetime' (v. 13). His reign coincided with periods of decline in both Egyptian and Mesopotamian empires, and, with his geographical position controlling trade routes between the two, he probably was the richest king at the time.

4 A wise division

1 Kings 3:16–28

We are now presented with an archetypal story illustrating and confirming the wisdom that Solomon has requested and been granted. Although English translations call the women 'the one' and 'the other', the Hebrew leaves them both nameless, often referring to them as either 'the prostitutes' or 'the women'. Even their speech consists of nearly verbatim quotes of each other (v. 22). All of this serves to enhance their anonymity and highlight the difficulty in deciding between two otherwise indistinguishable litigants.

Solomon cuts through this conundrum—not, in the end, with his sword, but by demonstrating that he has divine ability to distinguish good and evil. Peter Leithart observes:

Solomon's wisdom is not 'outside law,' yet neither is it a simple application of a rule. Unlike Adam, who took the fruit from his wife, Solomon listens to the women with discernment and judges rightly. Even more, Solomon enacts a judgement that exposes the hearts of the two women, showing his divine ability to 'distinguish good and evil'.

1 & 2 KINGS, P. 45

Although both Adam and Solomon 'listened' to the women who spoke to them (see Genesis 3:17), Adam did not listen to what God had commanded him previously. Because he ignored God's voice, he had nothing to bring to the table when he found himself needing to discern what Eve was saying. Thus, he ended up slavishly following her into the folly of the serpent's words, rather than intervening in the serpent's deception of Eve.

Solomon, likewise, hears the women's complaint, but his response is not dictated by what he hears. He takes on board not simply what the women present to him, but also their reaction to the divine litmus test that he brings to them. Like Abraham, whose heart God tested with another blade lifted over another son (Genesis 22:10), the women respond in a way that reveals their hearts. As in the story of Abraham, Solomon stays the blade, discerning the true mother and the true fear of God.

5 Dedication of the temple

1 Kings 8:22–53

The temple is to be the focal point of the prayers of the nation, of foreigners, and even of the Israelites in exile, yet it is emphasised that God cannot be contained in the temple. Rather, he is asked to 'hear from heaven' (v. 30). In fact, the reason for keeping the carrying poles on the ark of the covenant at all times (see v. 8) was to dispel the idea that God had been domesticated or entrapped in the temple (Terence Fretheim, *1 & 2 Kings*, Westminster John Knox, 1999, p. 44).

In his prayer for the temple's dedication, Solomon makes several requests of God. His first request concerns a situation where there is an accusation with no witnesses. He delegates this type of case to God himself, realising that even with the God-given wisdom he used to settle the case between the prostitutes, he cannot decide.

One of Solomon's more striking requests is for God to answer the prayers of foreign nations (vv. 41–43). This harks back to the Abrahamic covenant in Genesis 12:1–3 (Paul House, *1, 2 Kings*, Broadman & Holman, 1995, p. 146). There, Abraham and his seed were promised that they would be a blessing to all nations. Now, Solomon continues the fulfilment of the promise by making the temple a conduit for all people to 'fear God', as Abraham was shown to do (Genesis 22:12). The answers to foreigners' prayers in turn become a proof that the temple truly bears God's name or reputation.

In verses 46–51, we find Solomon praying for a hypothetical situation in which God's people have sinned and, as a result, have been taken captive. This prayer is actually directed at two audiences. Within the story, it becomes a warning to the people of Solomon's own day to take seriously the holiness of the God who resides among them, but it is also directed at the first readers of the book of 1 Kings. This was the generation that actually found themselves in exile. For them, it is a reminder of how they can have their relationship with Yahweh restored. Once again, they are reminded that God resides in heaven and can hear them wherever they go—even if the temple bearing his name, towards which they were to pray, has been destroyed.

6 The queen of Sheba

1 Kings 10

Sheba is probably Saba, in modern-day Yemen, and was down the coast from where Solomon had begun a shipping industry at the Gulf of Aqaba (9:26). The queen travelled around 1500 miles to see Solomon, and, later, Jesus would hold her up as a model of the price required in terms of dedication to seeking wisdom (Matthew 12:42).

Although Solomon exceeds his reputation in answering her riddles, it is his implementation of that wisdom in organisation and even worship (10:5) that takes her breath away. Indeed, the king's wealth and wisdom have become conspicuous. Thus, in both word and deed, his life points to a power beyond mere human capabilities.

The queen reflects this in her praise to Yahweh (v. 9). She uses God's covenantal name and reserves her highest remarks for God, not Solomon. For example, she not only attributes Solomon's qualities to God's favour but also sees the broader implications of that favour. Yahweh must love not only Solomon (see 2 Samuel 12:24) but his servants too. Indeed, he must love all Solomon's subjects, to have set him as king over them. In fact, it is God's *eternal* love for Israel that motivates his enthronement of Solomon. He desires that the people will be blessed not only in their lives but in their legacy—with one of the wisest and richest kings ever. In all this, Solomon's conspicuous wealth and wisdom engender praise not of their possessor but of their source.

The queen, like King Hiram of Tyre (1 Kings 5:7), makes a proclamation about how Solomon's wealth is to be used (v. 9). One of the ironies of wisdom is that a person requires wisdom to attain it. This suggests a dramatic contrast with Eve, who thought she could attain it with a simple plucking of fruit (Genesis 3:6). That which is gained cheaply usually proves its price. Wisdom needs to be exercised, so the queen adjures Solomon to use it for its intended purpose—to establish justice and righteousness, the very purpose for which Solomon requested it in the first place (3:6–9).

Guidelines

With life as pressured as it is, we often have our eyes fixed on what we need just to get through the day. Sometimes, our problem isn't that our desires are selfish, but that we do not trust God enough to make the big ask. Are we simply seeking for our material needs to be met, as if God were on a budget? In what areas could we have a more farsighted view, seeking God's wisdom in order to bless others?

Solomon was known as the 'beloved' of God, and yet, for all his laudable achievements, his record was tarnished by two shortcomings. First, he allowed worship to continue at the high places, and second, he bound himself in intimate relationships with those who did not worship God. Even everyday pastimes and relationships have the potential to turn our hearts toward themselves. In what ways are we checking the pull they might be exerting on our hearts?

Not only was Solomon known for his wisdom, but also he gives us an example of what it looks like in action. When have we paid attention simply to the image that people present of themselves? In which relationships are we being prompted to 'test the spirits' and allow God to illuminate people's hearts in response?

The first readers of 1 Kings were probably in exile. The warnings that had been put to King Solomon, and the consequences of ignoring those warnings, must have really hit home. And yet, Solomon offers hope in his prayer, that God would see even those in exile and hear their prayers. Do we feel exiled, cut off from God or the people who used to encourage us in the faith? God is still in heaven and he still hears. Will we turn to him despite the distance we feel?

The queen of Sheba is an example of someone who seeks wisdom and its source. In what ways might we invest in seeking and employing wisdom? What are we willing to do, how far are we willing to go, to get it? What is the cost for us to gain it—lost hours of entertainment, the risk of offending someone, the possibility of looking silly? How can our exercise of wisdom become a conspicuous part not only of our praise but of our witness to God's own wisdom and love? How can we worship God through displaying wisdom?

1 The fall and death of Solomon

1 Kings 11

Solomon is recorded as having fallen far from the exalted status he once enjoyed with God, a situation that is all the more tragic because it was not inevitable. In flagrant violation of Deuteronomy 7:3–4, he has married many foreign women; he has flouted Deuteronomy 17:14–20, which adjures kings to accumulate neither wealth nor wives and to remain close to the people they rule.

This all leads Solomon into a curiously motivated idolatry. As Paul House observes, 'In the ancient world polytheists tended to worship the gods of nations who had conquered their armies or at least the gods of countries more powerful than their own. Ironically, Solomon worships the gods of people he has conquered and already controls' (p. 167). Notably, the first foreign deity listed (v. 5) is the Canaanite goddess Ashtoreth. As Solomon no longer follows God wholeheartedly, the influence of this fertility goddess on his behaviour becomes evident.

Solomon's life is spared and the kingdom is not taken away completely, but this is due to his father's faith, not his own repentance (vv. 12–13). This demonstrates the power of faithfulness to trump sin, preserving both life and legacy. However, Solomon does experience some form of personal retribution for his breaking of the covenant with God. He gains enemies in the south-east (Edom, v. 14) and the north (Syria, v. 23), as well as in his own kingdom (v. 26). In all these cases, we find that the new ruler in Egypt has no qualms about fostering rebellion against Solomon. The old Pharaoh was the father of Solomon's Egyptian wife, but the new king has no desire to preserve the relationship, rendering Solomon's political marriage fruitless.

At Solomon's death, we find the evaluation formula seen so often in 1 Kings, taken from an as yet unknown source, 'the annals of Solomon'. The length of the king's reign, in this case, demonstrates God's faithfulness to his promise of long life. However, although he was initially wise and humble in both political and spiritual matters, he also displayed an obsession with women and prestige, and ultimately became disloyal to the covenant through idolatry. As Paul House says, 'he thereby serves as a warning to those who take their God-given gifts for granted or, worse, come to believe they have achieved greatness on their own' (p. 174).

2 Jeroboam and the golden calves

1 Kings 12

The division between the two kingdoms of Israel (north) and Judah (south) had been brewing long before the break. With forced labour projects and higher taxes in the north all benefiting the south, the relationship between the two groups was strained. Paul House points out, 'Only spiritual commitments could keep the nation united, and those commitments had already been weakened by Solomon' (p. 178). When a powerful ruler no longer reigns, rebellion rises swiftly.

Jeroboam (the leader of the ten northern tribes), realising that the traditional yearly pilgrimages to the temple in Jerusalem might undermine his new state, builds altars in the far north, at Dan, and the south, at Bethel (v. 29). The golden calves that he sets up are meant to depict Yahweh, not pagan deities. They are probably linked to the one built by Aaron on Mount Sinai, which Aaron claimed to be 'the God who brought them out of Egypt' (Exodus 32:4). This, however, breaks the second commandment, if not the first. Despite having plenty of Levitical priests, Jeroboam replaces them with priests from the ten tribes, and sets the Feast of Tabernacles back a month—probably to fit in with the later, northern, harvest. These changes not only separate the kingdoms but also prevent the northerners from worshipping Yahweh properly.

Although verses 8–16 lay the blame for the split at Rehoboam's feet, for listening neither to the elders nor to his subjects, verse 24 has the prophet Shemaiah claiming that it was the Lord's doing. It could be argued that God caused Rehoboam to ignore the elders' advice, but that would undermine his free will and doesn't explain why the episode is included here. Solomon's sin is the ultimate cause of the split, but the details of the immediate cause serve to teach a lesson in wisdom. Solomon's wisdom helped him to adjudicate in others' problems, but it was unable to fix his heart to Yahweh, nor was it automatically transferred to his son. The power to govern well is seen in the way we listen—not just to those who have problems for us to solve, but to those who oppose us, those who advise us and, ultimately, to the God who gives us both the position and the wisdom in the first place.

3 A prophet from Judah

1 Kings 13

The prophecy of Josiah's birth is one of only two Old Testament prophecies (the other being Isaiah 44:28—45:1, about Cyrus) to predict by name a king who will rise to power centuries later. In Josiah's case, it happened about 300 years afterwards. The prophecy is not only a precursor of his role in 2 Kings; it also signals the downfall of Jeroboam's current reign.

Jeroboam first tries to silence the 'man of God' and then to bribe him, but the prophet refuses, saying that he is not to eat or drink and must 'not return the same way [he] came' (v. 9). According to Jewish scholar Uriel Simon, this latter phrase is a common Old Testament idiom for 'be different' or 'avoid past mistakes'.

The 'man of God' becomes an unwitting symbol of Jeroboam in that, like him, he fails to trust in God's initial word. God promised Jeroboam a lasting dynasty like David's (11:38), and yet he feels the need to 'secure' it through religious and political manipulations that contradict the very one who promised him the throne in the first place. Likewise, the 'man of God', despite having witnessed God's power, does not trust God's full revelation. This was the case with the exilic audience of 1 Kings as well, who, despite having received a land, a dynasty and God's blessing, did not trust God, but rather hedged their bets, relying upon many deities and foreign alliances to secure their fate.

Interestingly, the 'old prophet' recognises what God has done through the 'man of God' and honours him in his death, both with proper burial and in seeking to be placed with him in death (vv. 30–31). The old prophet does not deem the man of God as utterly forsaken due to his lack of trust, but as one who was mightily used of God and at least spoke God's truth, if he did not always rely on it. This extends hope to the exilic audience, who, though they failed to trust God, have still experienced his power and spoken his word. They may be exiled but they are not forsaken, and, unlike the man of God, can choose to trust God's word again.

4 Jeroboam and Rehoboam

1 Kings 14:1–28

Jeroboam is punished for not following in the steps of David, who 'followed God with his whole heart' (v. 8). Ironically, of course, David transgressed as well, and part of his punishment was, like Jeroboam's, the death of his son. However, this represented the fruit of a single sin, whereas Jeroboam's continuing programme of sin led a whole nation away from God.

Of all the prophecies that Ahijah speaks against Jeroboam, the death of his son seems the most tragic. The boy is the only one of Jeroboam's family whom God finds good in, and he kills him. However, this son is spared the humiliation and fate worse than death that a lack of burial was considered to be in the ancient Near East (v. 13). Also, the suffering is relative: if this is the fate of the only good person in Jeroboam's family, the horrors that await the rest can only cause the reader to shudder. Finally, the short-term fulfilment of this prophecy stands as a guarantee that the long-term prophecies (covering a period of 200 years) will also come true.

Shishak's invasion of Judah marks the beginning of the 22nd Egyptian dynasty. His invasion was probably part of a wider operation, as the Karnak inscription describing the expansion of Egypt indicates. Shishak's humiliation of Rehoboam is clear from the emphasis placed (in verse 27) on the way the temple accoutrements and shields are replaced—with bronze rather than gold. The care given to these replacements (v. 28) reveals Rehoboam's concern to highlight the royal presence within Jerusalem, despite the loss of its former glory. Unfortunately, this does not demonstrate a change in the king's heart to a proper concern.

That concern should have been, according to the author of 1 Kings, the loyalty of the people to Yahweh. Sadly, Judah seems worse at this point than the northern kingdom of Israel. Whereas the latter is practising Yahwistic syncretism (12:28), Judah goes the whole hog and fully engages with Canaanite practice (14:23–24). God gave Israel the Canaanites' land because of the Canaanites' idol worship—but this has now become the Israelites' own practice, putting them on shaky ground. These practices will show up continually, throughout the books of Kings, both in prophetic critique and in the evaluation of each king's reign.

5 Asa

1 Kings 15:9–24

Asa reigned in Judah around 910–869BC. This 41-year reign probably included a three-year co-regency with his son Jehoshaphat, perhaps when he became ill (v. 23). His religious reforms were so extensive that he even removed his grandmother as queen mother because of her idolatry. In fact, Asa was the product of a marriage between his father Ahijah and Ahijah's own mother, Maacah (15:2, 10). This sort of incestuous relationship was strictly forbidden (Leviticus 20:11; Deuteronomy 27:20), but it serves to demonstrate that Asa was not fated to follow in his parents' footsteps. His love of God helped him break free from the destructive patterns of idolatry and incest from which he came.

Asa was continually plagued by war with the northern kingdom. In fact, Baasha, the king of Israel, built up a fortified city, Ramah, a mere four miles from Asa's capital, Jerusalem. Not only was this a menacing move, and perhaps the first stage in a planned invasion of Judah, but Ramah also controlled the main road in and out of Jerusalem to Israel and the coastal plain. It would have been an eighth-century equivalent of the Berlin wall, preventing the Israelites from deserting to Judah (see 2 Chronicles 15:9) and reaching Jerusalem.

Notably, although 2 Chronicles 16:1–9 criticises Asa for bribing the Syrians to attack Israel (thereby giving himself a chance to remove the threat posed by Ramah), 1 Kings makes no mention of the incident. However, the Chronicles narrative serves to demonstrate a trend in Asa's behaviour, thereby providing a less direct but more poignant commentary than that found in the repetitive royal evaluation formulas. 1 Kings 15:11–14 records that Asa's heart was in the right place, because, despite not taking the high places away, he was fully committed to the Lord all his life. But the details of his story, as told by the Chronicler, make a different point. Just as he dealt with his political problems, so Asa dealt with his diseased feet by paying other humans to help him rather than appealing to God (2 Chronicles 16:12). Being committed to the Lord and experiencing or relying upon his power are two entirely different things.

6 Jehu, Zimri, Ahab and Jezebel

Upon the death of Baasha (16:6), which is brought about by the beginning of a series of military coups, a new dynasty arises. This one is led by the former king's chief general, Omri. Although the text is just as negative about his influence as about Baasha's, Omri was politically powerful. He built the new city of Samaria and made it his capital (v. 24). He stopped the wars with Judah, which were sapping the country's resources, and his 'might', mentioned in passing in verse 27, was quite impressive, with records from both Assyria and Moab mentioning his dynasty by name. This shows that the biblical authors evaluated the kings according to their loyalty to Yahweh, and not their political or economic achievements. In fact, these achievements often go unmentioned, unless they serve another purpose. For example, Solomon's material wealth and building projects are discussed (1 Kings 4—7) only because they demonstrate God's blessing and God's choice of the temple as the unique dwelling place of his name (ch. 8).

The Omrite kings are quite deliberate about their rebellion against the Lord. Omri reinstitutes Canaanite worship practices, building a house of Baal and Asherah poles, and then his son Ahab rebuilds their cities. In verse 34, the rebuilder of Jericho is recorded as losing two of his sons in the process. This fulfils the curse that Joshua laid upon the city (Joshua 6:26). Some commentators connect this curse with actual pagan practices, such as the 'foundation sacrifice', in which infants were placed in jars that were placed in turn within the stonework of the city walls. In any case, the curse fulfilment signals that those who raise up what God has brought down will have the children they have raised up brought down to death.

Despite the fact that the clan of Jeroboam has been destroyed, the Omrite dynasty that follows (especially Ahab), rather than rectifying Jeroboam's sins, becomes paradigmatic for the sins of the northern kingdom, just as Jeroboam was.

Guidelines

Solomon, the king of Israel's glory days, starts well but finishes poorly. Might we be shifting our sense of self-worth on to the gifts, positions, possessions or power we have received, rather than their source?

Alternatively, in what ways can God's blessings extend beyond our own lives? For example, how do we instil the words God has taught us into others? Do we draw out God's character in those whom we influence? Have we built a legacy that neither rests nor falls on the acts of our children?

In what ways do we allow our message to be compromised, as the 'man of God' did, either through hypocrisy or by rationalising a change in our view of God's attitude toward something?

Are there people in our lives who have spoken God's truth to us, and yet later fallen off the rails? Can we honour the way God has used them, without either condoning all their behaviour or dismissing them completely?

In what ways might we be like Solomon's son Rehoboam, who replaced his stolen gold shields with bronze ones? In a disaster, is our lost or tarnished reputation our first concern? Are we more focused on damage control than on the things we may have done that have left us outside God's will?

The influence of our parents is definitely powerful, but it need not be fully determinative of our own lives. Asa grows up in a family that doesn't fear God and practises both idolatry and incest, yet he becomes one of the godliest kings of Judah. Which practices from our background exert a draw upon us, or perhaps fail to elicit an appropriate sense of shock because they have been modelled to us as acceptable? Which aspects of our past do we need to break free from or seek a new perspective on, with God's help?

1 Elijah and the widow from Zarephath

1 Kings 17

Baalism, which flourished under the influence of Jezebel, the Tyrian-born queen of Israel, was the worship of a storm-god. The rainfall that Baal was believed to control was especially significant in an agrarian society, hence his popularity. However, there were times of drought in the land,

and these were explained by the myth as periods when Baal had been swallowed and subdued by Mot, the god of death. When the spring rains came, it was because Baal's sister Anat had defeated Mot and released Baal.

It is against this background that Elijah, whose name means 'Yahweh is my God', enters the scene. He first prays for a prolonged drought, in order to demonstrate the impotence of Baal. Upon God's orders, he escapes Ahab's wrath by retreating to a brook, east of the Jordan, where God uses ravens (birds that don't even feed their own young) to feed him.

Elijah is then sent to a widow who lives in Zarephath, which is in Sidon (Phoenicia)—the heart of Baal country and Jezebel's homeland. As Baal was considered to be dead during a drought, Yahweh's assistance of the widow signifies Yahweh's enduring life in stark contrast with Baal's cyclical dying and rising.

Notably, the woman is asked to take some of her last meal and give it to Elijah, before God promises to provide for her and her son. Proactive faith is required if she is to see God's deliverance. Not only does God provide food; he provides life as well. When her son falls ill, the woman fears that her sin is the cause of his sickness, and Elijah her judge, sentencing her son to die, but Elijah again seeks God's power and his honour. To save the family from famine, only to allow them to capitulate to disease, would undermine the point that God is making through Elijah.

This point was surely brought home to the book's first audience, reading this text in exile in Babylon, hundreds of years after the events recorded in 1 Kings 17. To them, for Yahweh to demonstrate his ability to preserve the prophet, the widow and her son from political persecution, famine and death—all in a foreign land beset with pagan image worship—is to say that Yahweh can protect and sustain them in such a land as well.

2 Showdown at the Carmel Corral

1 Kings 18

The term 'troubler of Israel' (v. 17) comes from Joshua 6:18 and 7:25 (see also 1 Chronicles 2:7), in the narrative where Achan takes some of the booty devoted to destruction under the Lord's 'ban'. By disregarding Yahweh, he brings 'trouble' on Israel, causing it to lose a battle to the tiny town of Ai. Although Ahab indirectly admits Elijah's (and thus Yahweh's) power by accusing him of bringing about the drought, Elijah places the blame back on Ahab for having, like Achan, spurned the covenant with the one who truly controls events such as rainfall and battles.

The desperate slashing that Baal's prophets inflict on themselves (v. 28) was a practice modelled by their high god El in his attempt to revive Baal from death (during the drought). The prophets also dance or 'limp' around the altar—the same word describing Israel's dancing (or 'limping') between two opinions. The prophets thus become a picture of the people's wavering commitments. Elijah's challenge in verse 24 is levelled more against their syncretism than against Baal worship *per se*. By contrast, Elijah does not waver but takes charge of the action (v. 30). By rebuilding the altar of the Lord with twelve stones and using the traditional name of Yahweh, Elijah reminds the people of their own history and of who it was that formed them as a people in the first place.

By asking for the four large containers of water to be poured three times over the altar (vv. 33–35), Elijah prevents any possible accusation that the sacrifice accidentally caught fire in the dry, drought-scorched climate. However, by opulently dumping so much precious water on the sacrifice, he also ends up sacrificing to God the very thing that the people want their god to provide.

As the Hebrew day begins in the evening (see Genesis 1:4–5), the time of the evening sacrifice (v. 29) signifies a new day. The Baal prophets have had their day, and now Yahweh will have his. This story does not simply prove Yahweh's transcendence over all other gods, but rather, as Fretheim notes, his immanence (Fretheim, p. 105). Yahweh answers prayers, preserves life and delivers rain. One final miracle, however, confirms his actions: he enables Elijah to outrun Ahab's chariot in order to prevent Ahab from taking the credit, either for Baal or himself.

3 The prophet whisperer

1 Kings 19

After Elijah has definitively defeated Jezebel's prophets, it seems strange to find him fleeing. In light of the miracles he had witnessed, why would he be afraid of her death threats?

Actually, the Hebrew text does not say that Elijah was afraid, but rather that 'he saw' (v. 3). What did he see? His prayer in verse 4 clarifies the matter: he does not mention Jezebel; rather, the people of Israel are the ones who seek his life. Additionally, although at least 100 other prophets of Yahweh remain alive, Elijah is truly the only one actively opposing Jezebel and Ahab at the moment. Israel has indeed turned from Yahweh, destroyed his altars and killed his prophets (vv. 10, 14). Although there is a temporary turning for some (see v. 18), the ruling house remains recalcitrant. Elijah realises that nothing has changed in the court of Israel. Nor is his prayer merely a display of histrionics, for Yahweh never contradicts his assessment.

Accordingly, Elijah feels that his life is futile, no better than the lives of his fathers—that is, the prophets who preceded him. Furthermore, as a prophet, he was a member of the divine council and one who participated in their deliberations. Like Moses, Jonah and the apostle Paul, however, he loved Israel and would rather die than testify against it. In light of what has happened, however, he is now required to do just that—hence his death wish.

But what about his flight? Does it not prove that he is afraid? There are many parallels in this story with the exodus, and one of the most relevant is that, in both narratives, the people of God, having just experienced God's deliverance, then fall into idolatry (Exodus 32). Hence, Elijah, like Moses in Exodus 33, heads to Sinai to encounter God directly. He leaves (literally, 'walks'), not out of fear but from determination, to get to Sinai and experience God's presence. There, the earthquake, wind and fire all accompany God's manifestation, but he is not 'in' them as Baal was considered to be 'in' weather-related phenomena. As Fretheim notes (p. 109), these events are but God's vanguard. It is the ensuing silence that beckons Elijah to meet face to face with God, restoring his calling to serve at God's pleasure, and not for the results he will see from his mission.

4 Ahab and the Arameans

1 Kings 20:11–43

On the heels of God's instructions to Elijah at Sinai, we might expect the war with Syria to go badly for Ahab. However, God comes to deliver him and prove himself both to the Arameans (Syrians) and to Ahab.

In verse 23, the Arameans conclude that they have been defeated because Israel's God is a god of the mountains (for example, Sinai, Carmel and Jerusalem). In fact, one of the early names of God, El-Shaddai, suggests this possibility. Thus, they seek to defeat the mountain god outside his home turf, where, they presume, Yahweh does not rule, and where the tactical situation is different: their chariots will now be at an advantage over Israel's foot soldiers. However, God shows that he reigns not only on the plain, but both in and outside Israel.

Ahab is initially shown listening to and obeying the prophet, and even displaying some uncharacteristic wisdom in refusing to boast (v. 11). Hence, one of the most difficult issues in this passage is the prophet's condemnation of Ahab for his mercy to Ben-Hadad, the enemy king he has defeated with Yahweh's help (vv. 34, 42).

The prophet's condemnation of Ahab's actions can be explained, if uncomfortably, by appeal to the 'ban' (v. 42). As Ahab is fighting a holy war, the spoils are under the ban, or devoted to Yahweh. Although other nations in the ancient Near East considered all wars to be 'holy wars', due to the close integration of their religious and political systems, it was not so with Israel. Yahweh neither condoned nor helped them in all the wars they conducted (see, for example, Numbers 14:43–45; Joshua 7:2-5; 1 Samuel 4). When he did get involved, he did so for reasons beyond simple political gain—usually to demonstrate his Lordship to Israel or the nations. Thus, for the Israelites to keep the spoils would undermine God's purpose in aiding their fight, as the nations could claim that Israel was in it just for the material gain. Hence, when Ahab settles for gaining (back) cities and market privileges, he undermines God's purpose of proving to the Syrians that he reigns over all the earth. Like the man killed for refusing to wound the prophet—that is, not obeying the word of the Lord—Ahab is sentenced to die.

5 Naboth's vineyard

1 Kings 21

Ahab's proclivity to sullenness and anger, seen in 20:43, resurfaces here and proves to be his undoing. This can be seen in the subtle differences between Ahab's conversation with Naboth and his later report of the conversation to Jezebel. First, Ahab reports that he commanded Naboth to sell his vineyard to him, whereas he had actually asked him, 'Let me have it' (v. 2). This casts Naboth's refusal as defiance. Furthermore, Ahab doesn't say that he offered Naboth a better vineyard; he only mentions a replacement. Again, this lays emphasis on Naboth's spurning of his royal prerogative rather than the declining of an offer. Finally, Ahab omits the real reason Naboth won't sell—the divinely appointed tribal inheritance rights. All of this casts Ahab in a defensive, helpless light, as a victim of Naboth's obstinacy. Ironically, however, Ahab's sulking demonstrates that he probably would not have perpetrated the subsequent horrific act on his own.

While Ahab waffles, a blatant disregard for Yahweh and his ways comes from the pagan Jezebel. She takes advantage of Ahab's weakness, assuming even his name and authority (v. 8), and turns it into brutality. While she accuses Naboth of 'cursing God and the king' (v. 10), in fact it is the king and queen who despise God's laws, putting their convenience above Naboth's divinely appointed inheritance rights, taking possession of the vineyard when it should have reverted to his family. Indeed, Jezebel's question to Ahab (v. 7), referring to his sullen behaviour, is deeper than it first seems: 'Is this how you act as king over Israel?' Elijah sums up the dangers of such marriages and alliances, saying that Ahab has 'sold himself to do evil in the eyes of the Lord' (v. 20).

The deferral of punishment, from Ahab to his sons, seems unjust to our ears. However, it takes into account the ancient sense of communal identity, as opposed to today's individualist sensibilities, and strikes at Ahab's legacy, which would have remained untouched if only he had died. Secondly, the deferred punishment hypothetically leaves room for his sons' response to Yahweh. If Ahab's judgement can be changed, so can theirs.

6 Ill-fated alliances

1 Kings 22:6–25

As Ahab prepares to battle his old foe Syria, we find an instructive glimpse into the world of the prophets of ancient Israel. Although Jezebel has hunted down the prophets of the Lord, there are still plenty of court prophets to consult, as only the 450 prophets of Baal were killed in 1 Kings 18:40 (see 18:4, 18, 40). Unlike Elijah, these constitute a professional caste of prophets supported by the royal court, who purport to speak for the Lord to the king (v. 11). When Ahab consults these prophets, they say what they are used to saying—what the king wants to hear (v. 13). So, although God puts a lying spirit in their mouths (vv. 22–23), this spirit does not coerce them to speak against their will. It merely confirms the direction in which they are already headed (compare the hardening of Pharaoh's heart, Exodus 10:1).

However, Jehoshaphat distinguishes Ahab's prophets from a prophet *of the Lord* (v. 7). Micaiah ben Imlah is such a prophet, operating independently of the trappings and pressures of the court, though well aware of its operations and having access to it.

When Micaiah is adjured by the messenger sent to summon him to court not to speak a negative word to the king, he somewhat nebulously claims, 'Whatever the Lord says to me I will speak' (v. 14). However, at court, he begins by saying just what the hired prophets do. Is he going against his oath? One key to understanding this is found in the content of Micaiah's vision. He speaks of witnessing, in the divine council, a spirit volunteering to be a lying spirit in the mouth of all Ahab's prophets, in order to deceive him. Hence, by taking up the words of the prophetic 'yes men', Micaiah is embodying, as was often the practice of prophets (see Hosea 1:2–3), not what the Lord was *saying* to Ahab about the battle but what he was *doing*. Ahab, however, wants Micaiah only to speak the truth, not embody it (v. 16). The fact that Micaiah subsequently reveals the divine plot to Ahab represents one last offer of grace extended by the Lord. Thus, even in lying, Micaiah has sought to reveal to Ahab the truth of God's plan, the condition and bent of the court prophets, and one last chance to listen to God.

Guidelines

The widow at Zarapheth presents at least two challenges to our faith. Despite being down to her last reserves, she demonstrates the faith to share. This response, made under pressure, has probably been built up through small decisions throughout her life. In what ways do we make a practice of generosity, rather than leaving it to momentary inspiration or a guilt-motivated reaction? Secondly, she represents someone outside the people of God, whom God chooses to bless over the people of God. Are we willing, with Elijah, to go to those outside the community of faith to see God at work?

It is easy to see the Israelites at Carmel as vacillating and compromised in their allegiances, but in what ways are we like them—of two minds? What things demand our attention and devotion, and vie with God for our hearts?

Elijah became very depressed when he measured the success of his ministry in terms of (the lack of) visible change in others. Although such change can be a good thing, it is, by its nature, not in our hands. In what better ways might we measure ourselves?

Ahab is not simply an evil character but a weak one. His lack of internal conviction and character lead to idolatry and the effective abdication of his role to his wife, Jezebel—through which he commits his most despicable acts. In what ways do our inner desperations open the door to evil in our lives? Do we get into relationships with people who are not healthy for us, because they bring strength to an area where we feel helpless? What things cause us to sulk, become obsessive, get disproportionately angry or give up prematurely? All of these things signal the points where we are vulnerable to being abused and where we need God's strength and perspective.

In the Bible, God is called a god of truth, and yet truth can be used in ways that do not honour him or his will (Ephesians 4:29). In what ways have we used the truth as an excuse to hurt others or manipulate our own advantage? How have we embodied the truth of what God says rather than simply stating it?

FURTHER READING

Terence E. Fretheim, *First and Second Kings*, Westminster John Knox, 1999.

Peter J. Leithart, *1&2 Kings* (Brazos Theological Commentary), Brazos, 2006.
    Leithart's introduction is a virtual *tour de force* delineating the trajectories in 1 and 2 Kings of all the major institutions of the Old Testament, ultimately seeing the books through the lens of the gospel. Not to be missed.

Paul R. House, *1, 2 Kings* (New American Commentary), Broadman & Holman, 1995.

Luke 5:33—9:50

Throughout this section, Luke is presenting us with the outworking of Jesus' 'Nazareth manifesto' (4:18–19). There are plenty of illustrations of him healing the sick and setting the prisoners free, but we are also provided with samples of his teaching, in the formal 'Sermon on the Plain' (which bears close resemblance to Matthew's Sermon on the Mount), in parables and through conflict with the Pharisees, enquiries from John the Baptist and engagement as a rabbi with his disciples.

We see Jesus' ministry spreading out, as he heals a Roman centurion's servant, enters the realms of the dead to raise the widow of Nain's son, exercises forgiveness towards a 'sinful woman' and demonstrates his power over a violent storm on the Lake of Galilee.

We are also being drawn into a deeper understanding of who Jesus is. His call and commissioning of the Twelve is a messianic activity that parallels the use of 'twelve' to symbolise the whole of Israel (see Joshua 4:1–4; 1 Kings 18:30–32). His provision of food in the desert for the hungry multitude echoes the work of Moses as he led people towards the promised land. So it is unsurprising that Peter declares Jesus to be 'the Messiah of God' (9:20). Jesus' identity is made clearer to the three disciples on the mount of transfiguration, but we are privileged hearers, for not even the rest of the Twelve are to know that he is God's Son, fêted by Moses and Elijah. More significant still, we begin to share the dark secret of his own destiny (9:21–22, 43–44), which the disciples cannot yet grasp. The challenge to us is: can we and do we understand the implications for ourselves (9:23–25)?

Quotations are taken from the NRSV unless otherwise indicated.

1 Fasting or feasting?

Luke 5:33–39

The previous two stories have involved probing questions from 'the scribes and the Pharisees' (see 5:21–24, 30–32). Luke describes the same order of events as Matthew and Mark in telling this next story, but he intensifies both the questioning of Jesus and the claim that Jesus makes for himself.

The questioning is intensified by Luke's account of who is speaking. In Matthew 9:14 it is 'the disciples of John [the Baptist]' who ask, whereas in Mark 2:18 it is 'people'. In Luke 5:33 it is 'they'; this could refer to the people at Levi's party, but it is more naturally read as the complaining 'Pharisees and their scribes' (5:30). Thus we understand that the opposition are pressing on with their critical investigation.

In the previous two episodes, Jesus first demonstrated his power to forgive sins, then exercised table fellowship with outcasts—thus gathering in the people of Israel, as the Messiah was supposed to do, as well as claiming that he had come to call 'sinners to repentance', in preparation for God's return as king. This latest question, although it may appear to be about the 'ritual practice' of fasting, also needs to be read in a messianic context. One of the anticipated activities of the Messiah was great feasting (14:15–24; Matthew 22:1–14). The question from the Pharisees was probably intended to elucidate whether Jesus thought the messianic banquet had already begun.

Initially Jesus' reply seems to affirm this view. The parallel with the bridegroom and the wedding feast could well be understood as referring to the presence of the Messiah with his people (vv. 34–35; see Revelation 21:2; 22:17). But, at the very moment when the Pharisees might sense that they have trapped Jesus into a public claiming to be the Messiah, their evidence fades, for Jesus goes on to speak about the bridegroom being taken away. That was not what was anticipated for their Messiah!

Once again, Jesus appears to be teasing the minds of these religious leaders, seeking to involve them and then open them up to new possibilities.

2 Get real!

Luke 6:1–11

Luke (like Mark but not Matthew) continues to describe the questioning of Jesus' legitimacy by the Pharisees. Although the scene has shifted from Levi's party to the cornfields, and the time has moved to the sabbath day, the connection is the focus on food and, even more (from the perspective of the Pharisees), the lax way in which Jesus seems to regard the law. This incident also indicates that wherever Jesus went, the Pharisees seem to have been following not far behind. It must have felt like having the paparazzi chasing him down!

From the Pharisees' perspective, the sabbath was a day for rest, with a total absence of work, as the covenant commandment indicated (Exodus 20:8–11). In order to protect people against the merest possibility of breaking this law, work had to be defined, and in the end the definitions became restrictive and obsessive. If you left a needle in the clothes you wore, then it became work. If you plucked and rubbed a few ears of corn on a sabbath day's walk, then you were reaping and milling. To the Pharisees, it looked as if Jesus didn't care about God's purposes and the coming of his kingdom. To Jesus, it was clear that they didn't know God.

More worrying still, their desire to honour God and protect people from unwitting sin was breeding an attitude of critical attentiveness— more concerned to catch people out and point out their failures than actually to help them. This attitude soon slips into self-righteousness, enjoying the fact that others have failed and you have caught them out.

The next incident—again an apparent breach of sabbath regulations in the eyes of the Pharisees—exposes this incipient danger in two ways. First, they are becoming ever more concerned about 'finding an accusation against him' (v. 7). Second, the outcome of the healing is deep anger and resentment towards Jesus, and indications of worse to come. Mark makes clearer than Luke that the Pharisees are already forming an intention to get rid of Jesus (see Mark 3:6). Thus, their desire to be seen as the protectors of the law and nation degenerates into a willingness to kill Jesus to maintain their own standing.

3 During those days...

Luke 6:12–19

How vague it sounds—'during those days'! Does this vagueness suggest that Luke's research has failed to identify a specific time and place for the incident? Whatever the answer, what he recounts is of the utmost significance.

Take the opening and closing sentences, in verses 12 and 19. The first underlines the significance of prayer for Jesus in Luke's Gospel. The second, I suggest, indicates the impact of his prayer relationship with God—or, to put it another way, the secret of the immense power of his ministry: 'for power came out from him and healed all of them'. Jesus does not act alone and he never claims to be powerful in his own strength. It is only the Father who enables him to fulfil his ministry. This was indicated by the 'Nazareth manifesto', too: Jesus was called by God and equipped by God's Spirit 'to bring good news to the poor' (4:18).

The core of this passage is equally significant. There are at least four indicators of the growing impact of Jesus' ministry. First, he has an enormous following, including *many* disciples (v. 17). Second, he is empowered to select twelve apostles (v. 13)—reminiscent of the twelve tribes. Thus, Jesus is reconstituting the true Israel. We have heard about the calling of some specific disciples (especially Peter and Levi), but this indicates a further step in the organisation of Jesus' followers, and probably reflects a messianic intention. Third, there is the geographical range of his ministry, including Jerusalem (the seat of religious purity and the site of the temple) as well as Tyre and Sidon (v. 17), which were really beyond the boundaries of religious acceptability. Finally, we can note the comprehensive nature of his healing ministry ('all of them', v. 19).

Luke points out that the crowds have not come only to be healed; they have also come to 'hear him' (v. 18). So while this passage summarises Jesus' ministry so far (and perhaps that is the reason for the vague phrase 'during those days'), it indicates that what follows will provide a perspective on the previous incidents. It is giving 'an orderly account', enabling the reader to make sense of the details, but it also prepares the way for the Sermon on the Plain, which is to follow. This will show us what the people heard as they listened to Jesus.

4 Blessings and curses

Luke 6:20–26

We have already learnt of a number of healings (4:31–41; 5:12–26; 6:6–11) and more will follow (7:1–17). We have also learnt of Jesus' synagogue teaching (4:14–30) and his controversial debates with the Pharisees (5:30—6:11). We have watched his progress as he builds his band of disciples (5:1–11, 27–28; 6:12–16). Now, it is time for an account of Jesus' teaching to his disciples.

There are two indicators of context for this section of teaching. The first is that there is 'a great crowd of his disciples and a great multitude of people' (6:17). The second is that they had come 'to hear him and to be healed' (6:18), and, by setting the words in this order, Luke seems to be prioritising the teaching over the healing.

The teaching is clearly addressed to his disciples (v. 20), but we need to be clear that this means the 'great crowd' of disciples, not only the twelve 'apostles'.

As in Deuteronomy 27—28, both blessings and curses are delineated in this passage, with four of each. Luke thus presents a much tidier and more succinct version of the Beatitudes found in Matthew 5:1–12, and he resituates the parallel set of curses. Matthew's curses don't appear until chapter 23, where they are directed against the scribes and Pharisees. In Luke, as in Deuteronomy, the people are offered a choice between blessing and curse, with very clear consequences. Another noteworthy observation is that Jesus, in contrast with Deuteronomy, emphasises the blessings by placing them before the curses. Deuteronomy emphasises the curses by presenting them chiasmically (curses, blessings, then curses again).

Tom Wright is insightful when he writes, referring to the covenant in Deuteronomy, 'Now, with the renewed Israel formed around him, Jesus gave them his own version of the same thing' (*Luke for Everyone*, p. 71). It is also fascinating to notice that Jesus adds a 'prophetic edge' to his lists. He associates his reconstituted 'Israel' with the prophets of old: their fates will be the same. In other words, Jesus implies that this new Israel, made up of his disciples, is the prophetic community for the end of the ages.

5 Free to love

Luke 6:27–36

The Jews in Thessalonica accused the early Christian community of 'turning the world upside down' (Acts 17:6–7). In other words, the Christians were radically disturbing the proper order of things. In one sense, that was an acknowledgement, albeit unintended, that God's kingdom was being implemented. Here, in these words of Jesus, we see the outline of this radical kingdom, which the disciples were seeking to proclaim and live out.

At the heart of Jesus' words is the challenge to 'do good to those who hate you, bless those who curse you, [and] pray for those who abuse you' (vv. 27–28). These are all examples of what it means in practice to 'love your enemies'. Clearly, here, 'love' is not a matter of warm feelings but of beneficial actions. That idea is made even more concrete in what follows—the challenge to show absolute magnanimity to those who insult us publicly or deprive us of our possessions (vv. 29–31). According to Jesus, it is not enough to accept insult and injury; we must respond with positive steps of kindness.

The second section (vv. 32–34) goes back to the beginning (with 'If you love…' and 'If you do good…'), but it focuses more on the motivation for loving and doing good, which includes two aspects. First, we are challenged that we should be clearly exceeding even the good behaviour of 'sinners'; second, more fundamentally, in loving our enemies we will be like God himself—'children of the Most High' (vv. 35–36).

One puzzle (other than how we might live this kind of life!) remains. When Jesus says, 'Your reward will be great', does he mean that we can expect ample benefits in God's kingdom—such as the privilege of sitting at the Father's right side and being given large areas of heaven to rule over and enjoy (see 22:28–30)? Or does he mean that the reward is simply that we will be like God himself?

6 Reversing the law

Luke 6:37–45

Lex talionis: these Latin words refer to the legal principle that those who do wrong should receive a punishment commensurate to the damage they inflict. Break someone's arm in a fight and get yours broken as punishment; murder someone and you will be killed. This is a strong biblical motif (see Leviticus 24:17–22) and was originally meant to stop an increasing cycle of revenge by *restricting* punishment to only the equivalent of the damage done. Here, Jesus seems to turn the principle on its head, saying that we can expect the same *good* treatment as we mete out to others (v. 37).

His words about not judging, and about forgiving and giving, suggest a radical approach to human behaviour, not only because they focus on good treatment rather than punishment, but on at least two other counts. First, they emphasise our internal attitudes—although we should not over-stress this aspect. Judging may include not only the thoughts in our minds but the pronouncements we make about others or even the recompense we demand from them, while forgiveness may involve not only a forgiving attitude but also a practical release of the other person from the obligation to pay us back for their debts. Second, by using the passive voice ('you will not *be judged*'), Jesus is probably saying that these matters should be referred to God, for him to deal with them: 'Do not judge others and *God* will not then judge you.'

However, the most radical component of this section is Jesus' claim that the response we receive will not be commensurate with our good behaviour but will far surpass anything we may do (v. 38). As Jesus said on another occasion, if we give up anything for the gospel's sake, our reward will be a hundredfold (Matthew 19:29; see also Luke 18:29–30). We are intended, I suggest, to take this 'divine generosity principle' as applying to the other issues too.

Finally, Jesus' parables indicate that we are not in any position to judge or withhold forgiveness from others. This too is part of the gospel. We are not, in fact, in a superior position, but, because we are secure in God's love, we don't need to claim the moral high ground anyway.

Guidelines

Jesus frequently engages people in conversation, starting where they are. He appears to draw them along, without necessarily confronting them directly with his claim to be the Messiah. Can we learn from Jesus about how to be effective witnesses for him in our own culture?

What are people's questions about faith? How can we move them towards engaging with Jesus? Do we always need to challenge them that he is the Son of God or Saviour of the world, or can these realities be presented to them later on?

We have seen that the Pharisees appeared more concerned with criticism than constructive support, even seeking the pleasure of catching people out (see Luke 5:29—6:11). Are there aspects of contemporary life in which the church runs the same dangers? How do we balance concern for God's way of life and 'his righteousness' with the need for compassion?

Even when Jesus makes very high demands on us (for example, asking us to forgive out enemies), there is still a 'gospel dynamic', for the rewards are enormous (6:35). How can we ensure that we have the same gospel dynamic when we make the case for Christian ethics?

Pray for those who speak publicly for the churches, that they may have truth, grace and generosity embedded in the way they present themselves and in what they say.

1   True faith

Luke 6:43—7:10

How difficult it is to discern a person's motives from their words or behaviour! It is equally easy to misrepresent others, using either their words or their behaviour as evidence. If verses 43–45 are about ensuring that our behaviour matches our claims and that we are not behaving as hypocrites, then verses 46–49 are about ensuring that our discipleship, too, is genuine. But the parable of the two house builders takes us a step further, bringing in the element of divine judgement. Whose life will stand the test not of fire but of flood?

As in Matthew's 'Sermon on the Mount', this parable ends the formal speech of Jesus to his disciples (compare Matthew 7:24–27), but it is helpful to view the subsequent miracle story through the same lens.

The centurion is presented as one who has produced good fruit ('he built our synagogue for us') out of the 'good treasure' of his heart, 'for he loves our people' (6:45; 7:5). His 'faith commitments' are being tested by life's circumstances, like the house builders in the parable. Moreover, his care for his slave suggests that his love for the Jews is not just an astute political move, but flows from his heart. He genuinely values even slaves and the Jewish people, which is doubly remarkable for a Roman centurion.

He turns to Jesus for help—but is this only a superficial cry of 'Lord,

Lord' (6:46) from a man in desperate need? Does he send the elders because, as a Roman, he feels that coming to Jesus in person would be beneath him? Quite the opposite: his amazing declaration that Jesus does not need to enter his house provides further evidence of the 'rightness' of the centurion's heart. (He may be aware that, by entering a Roman's house, Jesus could be compromising himself in the eyes of the Jewish people and making himself ritually impure.) And so he receives his reward for his generosity to God's people, pressed down and overflowing. His servant is healed and, even more profoundly and appropriately, he becomes an example of true faith in Jesus (7:9).

Although there is much more to this story than I have indicated, reading it in the light of Jesus' teaching helps us to understand why Luke might have felt that this was the correct place for it in his 'order'.

2 Jesus' compassion

Luke 7:11–17

Who are 'the poor' to whom Jesus brings the good news of God's deliverance (4:18)? The poor are the powerless. The Roman centurion, for all his privileges and power, was impoverished when his beloved servant was dying, for he could do nothing to save him. Jesus announced the good news that not only was his servant healed but also a Roman could have faith!

Now Jesus, his disciples and the crowd of followers see a funeral procession coming out of a small village called Nain. There are several intriguing features about this account. Initially, the focus of the story is on the dead man. Although Luke says that 'he was his mother's only son, and she was a widow' (v. 12), we do not know at what point this information became clear to Jesus. Presumably he could tell she was a widow as there was no husband mourning with her, as well as from her attire, but how did he know that the dead man wasn't her husband? Did he ask other people, did he have special insight, or, at the point of intervention, did he not know? Certainly, however, by the time he addresses the corpse, he can perceive that the body is that of a 'young man' (v. 14).

Jesus' own focus, though, is not on the dead man but on the woman. On seeing her, 'he had compassion for her'. In his words 'Do not weep', there is an implicit promise or claim that her son is not really dead (compare 8:52, with the mourners for Jairus' daughter).

Then, Jesus touches the bier—a very strange thing to do, in his culture. The dead body made the bier unclean, so why would a rabbi deliberately make himself unclean? But if the man is not finally 'dead', then the bier will no longer be unclean. Jesus has authority over the realm of the dead. His 'holiness' is stronger than the power of uncleanness. Touching the bier is not only his way of halting the procession; it is a prophetic act. For Jesus, this is an act of divine compassion. For the mother and son, it is an unbelievable gift, but for the crowd it is a sign, leading them to confess that Jesus is a great prophet and confirming Jesus' claim in Nazareth. The words, 'God has looked favourably...' indicate the time for God's deliverance.

3 Evidence that demands a verdict

Luke 7:18–28

This account centres on two verdicts—one which we are invited to make for ourselves and one that Jesus gives us.

This first is in response to a query from John the Baptist: 'Are you the one who is to come, or are we to wait for another?' (v. 19). This was coded language for 'Are you the Messiah, the one whom God will send to redeem his people?' John had called Israel to get ready for the Messiah, through repentance; he baptised people in preparation for the coming of this one (ch. 3). But was Jesus the Messiah? Jesus was something of an enigma. Where, for example, was his 'winnowing-fork' of judgement (3:17)?

Jesus' reply correlates with his sermon in Nazareth (4:18–21) and both affirms and clarifies for John the kind of Messiah he is. It may not be accidental that Luke positions John's enquiry soon after Jesus has healed a Roman centurion's servant and commended his faith. Wasn't the Messiah supposed to destroy such people? But there is also a challenge and encouragement to John, and his disciples: 'Blessed is anyone who takes no offence at me' (v. 23).

The second is Jesus' verdict on John the Baptist (vv. 26–28). Jesus is crystal clear about the significance of John the Baptist: no human being is greater. John is greater even than the prophets who preceded him—who, of course, included Moses (see Deuteronomy 34:10–12; these are the last words of the Torah and, therefore, profoundly important). John is the forerunner of the Messiah. Jesus' followers should never denigrate John the Baptist, for he is the fulfilment of the whole Jewish story.

However, as usual with Jesus, there is a very significant twist in his declaration: '... yet the least in the kingdom of God is greater than he' (v. 28b). Just as Nicodemus had to learn that even he, a leading Pharisee, needed to be 'born from above' (John 3:7), so any follower of Jesus is in a more privileged position than even the greatest (namely, John the Baptist) in the old order. In making this statement, Jesus is, in effect, claiming his messianic position, although he does not identify himself directly as the one who brings in the kingdom of God.

4 Friend of sinners

Luke 7:29–50

No sooner has Jesus acknowledged the gossip that he is 'a friend of sinners' (v. 34, meaning that he affirms them by sharing and enjoying their hospitality) than he proves the point. In this episode, he shows himself behaving as their friend—as their public supporter and defender of the accused.

Initially, however, he is not partying with the gluttons and drunkards, but with high society: 'One of the Pharisees asked Jesus to eat with him' (v. 36). So Jesus is willing to be the friend of Pharisees, too. No doubt, Simon was taking risks among his peers by inviting him—unless, of course, he is seeking to catch Jesus out. This motif is not obvious in this story (contrast 6:1–11), although verse 39 hints at it.

The party atmosphere becomes highly charged as a sinful woman, probably a prostitute, creeps in. Trying to work out the position of the protagonists is tricky, but it probably makes sense to think that Jesus' feet were behind him and to the side, so that he couldn't actually see the woman approach him. If Simon was in front of or to the side of Jesus (who, as his guest of honour, would sit on his left side), he could probably see the woman and recognise her. We can also imagine one of Simon's servants reporting her arrival with horror.

'Is Jesus a prophet?' This is either the question that Simon is seeking to answer in his own mind, or it refers to a claim that he is keen to disprove. The woman's voluptuous advances to Jesus answer Simon's question, but not as he expects. He thinks that if Jesus has prophetic powers, he will know all about this woman and, as a holy man, reject her—but Jesus' words and deeds show that he is a prophet and something more. Of course he knows that she is a sinner but also that she has now been forgiven. Jesus may even be hinting that he himself has power to forgive her (vv. 47–49; compare 5:20–25).

Jesus' parable and his challenging words are not only a successful defence of the woman and a clear indication of his prophetic gift; they are a penetrating attempt to open Simon up to the friendship and forgiveness of Jesus, too. As with Nicodemus, so here we see Jesus seeking the lost, including the Pharisees.

5 Invaluable women

Luke 8:1–3

Getting a correct understanding of Jesus' ministry is not as easy as we might think! In 6:13 we learn of Jesus selecting the 'twelve... apostles'; next we hear of 'a great crowd of his disciples' (6:17), and in 7:11 it is 'his disciples and a large crowd'. (There are also references to crowds without specifying any disciples.) Now we read, 'The twelve were with him' (v. 1). Does that mean they weren't present while he was speaking to John the Baptist's disciples? Were they eating with Simon too, or not?

Perhaps it is more important to understand that this is both a summary passage and one that Luke is using to provide us with a more complete picture. The summary tells us of the ongoing and spreading mission of Jesus. In using the words 'proclaiming' and 'bringing the good news', Luke is probably reminding us of 4:18–19 ('to bring good news to the poor... to proclaim the year of the Lord's favour'). The presence of the Twelve, being with him for this task, prepares us for their mission in 9:1–2.

Beyond these details about 'the twelve', though, the most striking point is the mention of the women—three of them by name. This gives us a more accurate idea of how Jesus' mission actually took place, for it was these women who provided for the group 'out of their resources' (v. 3).

Howard Marshall makes two fascinating points. These women, he says, 'appear on the same level as the men'. Personally I find this comment unconvincing, because they are distinct from the Twelve and certainly have a different role allocated to them. Marshall's second comment is significant, though. He rejects the traditional identification of Mary Magdalene with the sinful woman in the previous chapter. Although Mary is described as one 'from whom seven demons had gone out' (v. 2), he notes that 'demon possession and sinfulness are to be carefully distinguished' (see *The Gospel of Luke*, p. 316).

Why these three women (Mary, Joanna and Susanna) are mentioned by name is intriguing. Clearly Mary Magdalene was an important witness of the resurrection, as might be Joanna, if we assume she is the same person as is mentioned in Luke 24:10. Susanna is otherwise unknown to the Gospels. What they indicate is that Jesus had female followers (probably unusual for a rabbi: see Marshall, p. 317), who later became part of the Christian community (see Acts 1:14).

6   Liquorice allsorts?

Luke 8:4–21

A parable, an explanation, a saying and an uncomfortable incident! What is it that unites them, or is this a place where Luke has forgotten to be 'orderly'? Although these elements may appear very different, they are all linked by the topic of hearing and receiving 'the word of God'.

Luke's version of the parable of the sower (or, more accurately, 'of the soils'), with its explanation, is more concise than Mark's (4:3–8, 13–20) and Matthew's (13:3–9, 18–23) but contains all the essential details. All three Gospels place the story and its explanation on either side of a puzzling quotation from Isaiah 6:9–10. This quotation seems to imply that the purpose of telling parables was to hide the truth ('so that… they may not understand') but it may simply be describing the outcome. Noticeably, Luke omits the hardest part of the saying: 'so that they may not turn again and be forgiven' (Mark 4:12c).

We may be missing the nuance here. It is now generally agreed that the main focus of this parable is the amazing fruitfulness of the successful seed, rather than the failures of the others. If so, then Jesus is underlining the privilege of the disciples—they have truly seen and responded—

rather than the failure of the majority to grasp his message.

Luke, however, does also seem to want to emphasise a distinction between the crowd and the true disciples. There is mention of 'a great crowd' and 'the crowd' in verses 4 and 19 respectively, and he drops the reference to 'those who were around him' that we find in Mark 4:10, thus emphasising the privileged status of the disciples who hear the parable's explanation. This distinction is underlined by the saying about his true family, in verse 21.

What remains undeniable is that Jesus is very clear about the need not to follow him out of interest but to listen to God through him, to live in the light of what we hear and then to stay committed for the long haul. Luke's treatment of both the need to listen properly and the benefits of doing so seems to clarify this point (vv. 16–18; compare Mark 4:21–25).

Guidelines

The Roman centurion provides an illustration of someone being drawn into the faith community who would normally be regarded as beyond it. In some ways he is a precursor to Cornelius in Acts 10. Are there people around us who are in similar positions (men with churchgoing wives, who don't attend but are willing to help out; people who donate to the work or preservation of the church; those who find a sense of mystery and peace when they visit cathedrals; those who seek 'baptism' for their children)? How do we distinguish those who are simply crying 'Lord, Lord' from those who are open to God's kingdom? Pray for people you know in this 'liminal' position.

In this week's readings, there are several indications of the way Jesus related to women (see 7:11–17, 36–50; 8:1–3, 19–21). Is there anything that disturbs you about his approach? Is there anything we can learn? Do we need to reshape our mission accordingly?

The parable of the sower alerts us to the fact that not all will respond positively or permanently to the message of Jesus. Do we still use ways to 'broadcast' the seed of the gospel (such as christenings and funerals, school assemblies, parent-and-toddler groups, gatherings for older people or visits to care homes)? Would it be appropriate to place adverts in papers? Can we use social media as a vehicle? How does your church take the kinds of risks, in sowing the seed, that this parable indicates?

Does this parable also suggest we should focus on discipling and nurturing those in whom the word generates and grows, to ensure that we get a good harvest eventually? How might we do this more effectively?

1 The storm on the lake

Luke 8:22–25

Where is the real storm? Where is the real danger? Luke has no doubt that the physical storm is real enough ('The boat was filling with water, and they were in danger', v. 23), but the real storm is inside the minds of the disciples. The ultimate danger is that their faith is failing them.

It makes sense to see this as an episode in which the disciples experience the truth of the sayings 'To those who have, more will be given' (8:18) and 'To you it has been given to know the secrets of the kingdom of God' (8:10). They have faith; they have responded to the call of Christ to follow, and they have been selected to be his closest companions. Now, through this experience on the lake, their faith will grow, but so will their awareness that following Christ is a dangerous business.

There is little doubt that Luke presents us with a group of terrified disciples ('Master, Master, we are perishing!') but, equally, with a group whose instinct is to turn to Christ. The most noticeable feature, however, is the revelation that comes to the disciples through the calming of the storms (on the lake and in their own understanding). Through their ordeal, a question arises in their minds: 'Who then is this…?' It will be formally answered by Peter a chapter later (9: 20), but emotionally it has already been answered, for the words 'They were afraid and amazed' indicate an awareness that they are in the presence of God. No longer does their fear relate to the physical danger around them; it relates to their sense of being in the presence of God, the most dangerous place for a human to be. Like Isaiah, they recognise, 'Woe is me! … my eyes have seen the King, the Lord of hosts!' (Isaiah 6:5).

The disciples have seen the impact of the coming of God's kingdom in the midst of a life-threatening situation. They have experienced what it means to be protected as Christ's brothers and sisters. They have also discovered that such protection does not always mean a felt sense of safety or of the immediate attention of Christ—but he will act decisively (compare, for example, Acts 4:23–31).

2 Discernment

One key to understanding this passage is to think in terms of discernment. First we note, 'Now when Jesus returned, the crowd welcomed him' (v. 40). This 'welcome', presumably back to Galilee (see 8:26), is in marked contrast to the previous episode, where the people of the Gerasenes 'asked Jesus to leave them' (v. 37). There, they were afraid because the restoration of the demoniac had cost them dear (v. 33). Probably, though, and even more significantly, the source of their fear was their anxiety about his powers and what the source of those powers might be.

After the storm on the lake and in the demoniac's life comes this welcome—relative tranquillity—but not for long. Soon there is a desperate request for Jesus to heal Jairus' dying daughter. Then comes the challenge of moving through the crowd, which 'pressed in on him' (v. 42), and the draining of his power as the woman with the haemorrhage is healed. This story is full of dramatic tension but it also underlines the fact that Jesus' compassion is available to all. Both of the people in need of his healing indicate Jesus' concern to bring good news to 'the poor'. The woman was unclean as well as female, and Jairus' daughter was still a child—again, one of the most vulnerable classes in Jesus' time. In addition, she was perceived to be unclean by the time he reached her, for she was a corpse.

Both incidents are used by Luke to display Jesus' discernment. First, he senses that power has gone from him in the healing process. The woman's confession prompts his discerning comment, 'your faith has made you well' (v. 48). The second example is his declaration to the mourning women, 'She is not dead but sleeping' (v. 52).

The courageous insight of Jesus is emphasised in both incidents by the strength of opposition brought against him—first, Peter's disparaging comment that everyone in the crowd is touching him (v. 45), and then the mocking laughter of the wailing women (v. 53).

Even more than discernment, these two healings and the prior deliverance underline the immense authority and power of Jesus to fulfil his Nazareth calling. 'The Spirit of the Lord' is certainly upon him and he is proving it as he brings 'good news to the poor'.

3 Expanding the impact

Luke 9:1–9

We have been presented with a Jesus who has God-like powers, calming the storm, delivering the possessed man, healing the woman whom all the doctors had failed to help, and raising a dead child. Now the ministry of the kingdom is to be extended by releasing his disciples into his work. Not only can he exercise kingdom power, but he can disperse it.

Jesus 'gave them power and authority over all demons and to cure diseases' (v. 1). If we are to read Luke's Gospel correctly, however, we must note that, while the demonstrations of Jesus' power over nature, the demonic world and sickness are presented very vividly, in themselves these demonstrations are not the core issue. Three times within ten verses, Luke emphasises the priority of proclaiming the kingdom: 'He sent them out to proclaim the kingdom of God and to heal' (v. 2); 'They departed... bringing the good news and curing diseases everywhere' (v. 6); 'He... spoke to them about the kingdom of God, and healed those who needed to be healed' (v. 11).

In no way are healings and deliverance unimportant to Luke, but their importance is within the theological framework of the coming of God's kingdom. They can all properly be seen as evidence of the coming of this kingdom, but they are not understood correctly, or even at all, apart from it (see 4:43–44). In this sense they are not 'random acts of kindness' or even 'random demonstrations of Jesus' power'. They are, at the very least, 'signs of the kingdom'. Even more, they are victories of the coming kingdom, for they are taking control away from Satan and restoring God's order, God's *shalom*. Here, too, it is true that to those who have, more will be given, for those who see in Jesus the bearer of the kingdom will find that insight confirmed. But to those who have not, particularly his opponents, even what they have will be taken away. They will only see evidence of Jesus' involvement with Satan.

The implied success of the Twelve in carrying out Jesus' commission (9:10) demonstrates the growing impact of the kingdom, but the introduction of Herod's machinations casts a dark cloud over the growth of this kingdom. It reminds us that the territory is contested. 'John I beheaded,' says Herod (v. 9). Now he wants to see Jesus, too.

4 Knowing the secrets of the kingdom

Luke 9:10–20

If there is any one incident in the Gospel that can claim to be the fulfilment of the 'parable of the sower', it is surely the feeding of 'about five thousand men' and, presumably, an even larger number of women and children. Handing out food to this vast crowd was like casting seed over a large field. There was no discernment about who had faith enough to be healed, no enquiry into their level of responsiveness, not even a check as to whether they properly appreciated how and where the food came from.

The miraculous feeding is an act of astounding power as well as generosity, but what does it mean? The messianic implications of the event are explored in detail in John 6, but the construction of Luke's Gospel here may well echo John's Gospel (or, more precisely, the sources that underlie John's Gospel). In John, at the end of the account of the feeding and the debate about Jesus' claim to be the 'bread of life' comes Peter's declaration, 'You have the words of eternal life. We have come to believe and know that you are the Holy One of God' (6:68–69). The title 'Holy One of God' is probably to be understood as a messianic title. In Luke, immediately after the feeding miracle, we hear Peter's confession that Jesus is 'the Messiah of God' (v. 20).

Given this similarity between the Gospels, it is worth noting some other features. First, the conversation in Luke takes place 'with only the disciples near him' (v. 18); similarly, in John's Gospel (although John presents it rather differently), Peter's 'confession' emerges when the disciples are left alone with Jesus (John 6:67). Secondly, the answers to Jesus' question 'Who do the crowds say that I am?' in Luke 9:19 summarise the views expressed in the long discussions in John's Gospel.

So, while it would be wrong to claim that Luke is using John's Gospel, at the very least both Gospels indicate a similar kind of process, each ending with a profound declaration by Peter about Jesus' identity.

5 Growing mystery

The transfiguration represents, among many other things, God's view of Jesus as his beloved Son and chosen one (v. 35). The cloud represents the presence of God, hidden from human observation (see Exodus 19:18–19).

This is the fourth perspective on Jesus that we have been offered in this chapter—as though Luke is stimulating his readers to form their view about Jesus. First, we have had the political view of Herod, who is 'perplexed' (9:7). He knows the rumours that are circulating among the people, all of which imply that someone has come back from the dead (John the Baptist, Elijah, or one of the prophets: 9:7–8, 19). These represent the second perspective. Narratively, Herod's reflections on these rumours serve to raise our interest in Jesus.

Third, we have the view of the disciples, Simon Peter in particular, who describes Jesus as 'the Messiah of God' (v. 20). (Matthew 16:16 adds, 'the Son of the living God'.) Finally, in verse 35 we have the decisive view—God's view.

We have heard the same thing at Jesus' baptism, in Luke 3:22. There, Luke presented Jesus as being probably alone—praying after his baptism, and hearing a voice that said, '*You* are my Son'; by contrast, Matthew 3:17 says, '*This* is my Son' in a more public setting. So Luke does not make it clear how public the statement is: perhaps we have been let into a secret. Earlier, Mary has been told the same thing by the angel Gabriel (Luke 1:35)—again, in a secret encounter to which we, as readers, have privileged access. Even here at the transfiguration in Luke, the statement is almost secret. Only the three chosen disciples hear the divine voice, and they are commanded to keep it to themselves. Unlike most people who receive this command to silence, they obey (v. 36)—so now, at least, the secret has been entrusted to faithful witnesses.

The next time we hear these words, or something like them, will be in the trial scene before the Sanhedrin (22:70). It is Jesus' relationship with his Father that is the ultimate reason for his crucifixion, but we, the Gospel readers, need to know that it is a reality, rooted in his conception and affirmed by God. It is not a false claim made by Jesus; it is not blasphemy, as the Sanhedrin will claim. It is God's truth.

6 'Faithless and perverse'

Luke 9:37–50

'Faithless and perverse' (v. 41) are very strong words, representing a harsh criticism by Jesus, but to whom are they spoken? There are three possible unfortunate candidates! First is the boy's father. He is the most visible person at this point in the narrative, and, immediately after this pronouncement, Jesus addresses him again. In Mark's version, it is most natural to read it this way because of the connection with the Father's plea, 'I believe; help my unbelief!' (Mark 9:19, 24). But it is strange to refer to one person as 'a generation'. The condemnatory tone also runs counter to the usual compassionate approach of Jesus to suffering people, which is exemplified here again in the words 'Jesus… gave him back to his father' (Luke 9:42).

The second possibility is the disciples. This, again, would be a natural reading, because the words immediately preceding Jesus' verdict tell us that the disciples have failed to deal with the possessed child: 'I begged your disciples to cast it out, but they could not' (v. 40). In Mark's version (though not Luke's), the disciples ask later why they failed, and Jesus tells them that they needed to fast and pray. Perhaps, like the Israelites while Moses was on the mountain, they have not been keeping the faith properly (Deuteronomy 9:11–21).

The third candidate is the whole crowd. This is the most natural understanding of the word 'generation', which would perhaps include the father, the disciples and everyone else. In this case, the whole scene underlines for Jesus the waywardness of everyone around him.

It seems probable to me that what prompts Jesus' strong reaction is his awareness that 'the Son of Man is going to be betrayed' (v. 44) and 'must undergo great suffering' (v. 22), for he has just been discussing with Moses and Elijah (both of whom had to deal with 'faithless and perverse generations') 'his departure, which he was about to accomplish at Jerusalem' (v. 31). In other words, the need of the child, the desperation of the father, the failure of the disciples and the intrigue of the crowd all underline for Jesus the inevitability of his suffering.

Guidelines

On at least two occasions, Jesus challenges the disciples about their lack of faith or their faithlessness (see 8:25; 9:41). These are disciples who have confessed that Jesus is the Messiah (9:20) and have been involved in very powerful mission activities, including healings (10:9, 17).

Reflect on aspects of your life and the life of your church where similar challenges might be warranted—for instance, the need to raise money for mission, the need to provide the right calibre of leadership, anxiety about how God might sort out a relational problem, doubts over your ability (even with God's help) to fulfil some task. Think about people or situations that seem to diminish your faith because fear takes over, as it did for the disciples during the storm—for example, news of a serious illness or redundancy. Pray for yourself and others in your church who need 'faith' strengthening.

Similarly, reflect on issues in your life and the life of your church where your behaviour might betray a lack of complete integrity in following Christ. Do we need to stand against decisions that take away resources for the vulnerable? Do we invest enough of ourselves in supporting those with mental illnesses or the diseases of old age, especially dementia? Are there more direct ways in which we indicate our waywardness from Christ? Pray for any situations and people who face these challenges.

Do you think Christ's apparently harsh words were mainly criticism or mainly meant to stimulate faith and faithfulness? How can we help people in their times of weakness?

FURTHER READING

E. Earle Ellis, *The Gospel of Luke* (New Century Bible Commentary), Eerdmans, 1974.

I. Howard Marshall, *The Gospel of Luke* (New International Greek Testament Commentary), Paternoster, 1979.

John Nolland, *Luke 1—9:20* (Word Bible Commentary), Word, 1989.

Tom Wright, *Luke for Everyone*, SPCK, 2001.

Isaiah 1—12

Isaiah lived in Jerusalem in the second half of the eighth century BC. The earliest historical reference is the death of Uzziah (Isaiah 6:1), somewhere between 742 and 735, and the last is 701, when the Assyrian king Sennacherib invaded Judah. That is a long period of ministry, through significantly changing times, and it is not always easy to decide where a particular oracle fits into the timescale. Beyond that, however, scholars agree that the book also includes a great deal of material that was written by others, long after Isaiah's own day, and that this later material is included not only in the second half of the book, from chapter 40 onwards, but also here and there in the first half as well.

At first sight, this makes it complicated to know how to read the text. Nowadays we are used to narratives progressing in a historical order—first oracles first—but clearly ancient authors had different ideas. To some extent, this makes it legitimate for us to read Isaiah in the way we typically hear it in church, with individual passages taken in isolation; there is nothing wrong with meditating on each day's reading as a self-contained piece. It is intriguing to try to find wider connections, but not essential. Furthermore, it means that these oracles were collected not with an eye to recording history but rather, in a way, to focus on their enduring value for later readers. The challenge we shall face, therefore, is to discern what that value might be in our world today, which differs so much from Isaiah's. The notes each day can give some broad outlines, but faithful reading requires application at the practical level by each individual or small group of readers in their own equally varied settings.

At the end of each day's notes, I have included two additional passages —one Old Testament, the other New Testament—that might be interesting to read in conjunction with the day's main Bible passage. Please consider this extra reading as optional!

Comments are based on the New Revised Standard Version of the Bible.

1 Be warned

Isaiah 1:1–9

The first chapter of Isaiah evidently stands somewhat on its own. There is a new introductory heading at 2:1, so we need to ask what this means for our present chapter. A likely answer is that chapter 1 serves as an introduction to the book that follows. It is not a summary, like a table of contents, however: there are several important themes, such as the king and the foreign nations, that receive no mention here. Rather, it is an introduction which invites us to read all that follows in deadly earnest.

Today's passage is focused on the reasons why Judah is to be judged, tomorrow's (1:10–20) on the emptiness of religion without justice but also on the offer of full forgiveness, while the final section (1:21–31) looks at the division between those who accept the offer of forgiveness and those who do not. In broad terms, this reflects the shape of the whole book in its three main parts (chapters 1—39; 40—55; 56—66). The aim is to invite us to recognise that although we may be in the first part now, we can be urged to move through to the positive aspect of the third if we respond wisely.

As we read the opening verses, therefore, we realise that this is not just a history lesson about Judah, when God judged her at the hands of the Assyrians (vv. 6–9) because of idolatry (v. 4). Rather, the underlying fault is one that occurs in every generation—taking all the good things that God has to offer while failing to acknowledge him directly, personally, and with the respect that a child should show to a parent who gives and provides without prior condition (vv. 2–3).

That fault led to judgement in the past, but we seem to be addressed directly by verse 5, which asks why, in the light of past history, we continue to behave in the same way as those in earlier times. Unchecked, this behaviour will lead to the same fate as they suffered. It was devastating, but not total: verse 9 reminds us that in his mercy God spared a few. Will we read on with a commitment to ensure that we are included in that remnant?

Optional reading: Amos 4:4–12; Romans 1:18–25.

2 Empty religion

One obvious response to the threat of invasion as a form of divine judgement is to try to be more 'religious'. Church attendance tends to increase quite markedly in times of national conflict, and it was no different in ancient Judah, but the practice of religion in isolation is met with a scathing expression of rejection in verses 11–15. It is difficult to imagine a more complete condemnation of any established form of worship than the catalogue here: everything that seems to be commanded in the law is now said to be unbearable to God, and it is sobering to substitute modern expressions of formal worship (whatever your favourite may be) for the sacrifices, temple attendance and observance of holy days in this passage.

It is difficult to suppose that Isaiah can mean that these practices are inherently wrong. After all, even prayer is included (v. 15). It is rather, as he moves on to explain, that religious observance is useless if it is not accompanied by a personal life that is both separated from evil and directed towards the care of the vulnerable and the pursuit of justice (vv. 16–17). Hands that are stained with the blood of murderous guilt cannot be effectively lifted to God in prayer.

That leaves us with a problem, however, for which of us could say that we match up to these high demands? We may well be aware of the dangers and still feel that we fall short. Does that mean we should give up on religious observance altogether? At this point, a glorious alternative is offered. Summoned to God's court, where we expect to be pronounced guilty (v. 18a), we find instead that forgiveness is on offer, albeit in a way that does not just overlook failure with some form of benign indulgence. Rather, the whole fabric of our being can be changed—from crimson to white.

Of course, as verses 19–20 make clear, it depends on our willingness to be changed. Forgiveness has to be accepted, which is not always easy to come to terms with. Unlike the times when our own use of liturgy becomes little more than formulaic, in the way that Isaiah condemned, God's words are never empty.

Optional reading: Isaiah 66:1–2; Matthew 23:23–36.

3 One by one

Following the open invitation at the end of yesterday's passage, we might have supposed that everyone would respond positively. Unfortunately, it remains the case that, unlike in the past golden age (v. 21), the fundamental principles of social justice are flouted by some in order to advance their own interests at the expense of the most vulnerable members of society. Note especially how the condemnation in verse 23 contrasts with the exhortations in verse 17.

This concern for justice is a building block of Isaiah's critique throughout the first part of the book, and we shall meet it again in different forms. It includes, but is not limited to, the restricted processes of the legal system, and we may profitably reflect carefully on the equivalents to those processes in today's world, whether at the international, national or local level. Imaginative interpretation is invited from every reader! In this passage we see that corruption will not be overlooked, even if justice is sometimes delayed; the vision is for such impurity to be removed as if in smelting, leaving only the tested and tried elements to be restored. Elsewhere we shall find that the concern for justice builds repeatedly into other elements of Isaiah's theology, so that it cannot be dismissed as an unimportant side issue.

From verse 27 on, we find that the inevitable outcome of injustice is a division in society—a relatively new idea in the development of thought in ancient Judah. As opposed to crude forms of judgement, such as military or natural disasters that affect everyone alike, there will be a distinction between those who repent and those who rebel (vv. 27–28). The end of the latter group is then described more elaborately using the image of fire, just as at the end of the book of Isaiah as a whole (66:24). Thus, the introduction to the book ends with an impassioned warning to respond positively to all that is to follow: read not only carefully but also responsively, for your ultimate destiny depends on your committed engagement with this text.

Optional reading: Isaiah 3:13–15; Matthew 7:21–27.

4 Swords into ploughshares

Isaiah 2:1–5

After the introduction in chapter 1, a fresh start is made here. An inspiring vision of the nation's ideal ultimate destiny is portrayed (vv. 2–4), and then, deliberately echoing some of the language of that vision, verse 5 exhorts us to 'walk' (that is, live and set our values) in its light. The continuation, from verse 6 on, shows how far short of this ideal the current situation falls. The vision thus serves both as an inspiration for future improvement and as a standard by which the failings of the present can be realistically assessed. In New Testament terms, 'all have sinned and fall short of the glory of God' (Romans 3:23).

The vision combines a glorious hope for Zion with consequences of a universal dimension. While 'Judah and Jerusalem' in verse 1 reflect current political realities, the vision sees the situation from the perspective of Zion as God's dwelling place. This image will have been familiar to the first readers from their use of the Psalms in their regular worship. Whereas Jerusalem and its temple nestled, physically, below more imposing neighbouring heights, the prophet anticipates a time when crude politics will be replaced with divine realities. In such a world, arbitration on the basis of God's instruction will replace international conflict, so that (in words prominently displayed today at the headquarters of the United Nations) armaments will no longer be needed, but the resources they devour will be turned instead into tools that make for peaceful prosperity (v. 4).

The language of verse 4 is a deliberate parody of the more familiar appeal, in times of war, to bring all one's iron implements to be turned into weapons: see Joel 3:10, which finds echoes in the behaviour of other nations around the Mediterranean. The one who controlled these resources controlled the arms trade, and could both get rich on its back and determine who would be the dominant regional power (see 1 Samuel 13:19–22). The vision for the reversal of this situation remains alive more than ever in today's world. Its realisation will come, however, not from simplistic idealism or gesture politics but from the implementation of the prior condition in verse 3. Hearts and minds need godly education in order to change vile behaviour. 'Come, let us walk in the light of the Lord.'

Optional reading: Joel 3:9–15; Ephesians 6:10–17.

5 The song of the vineyard

Isaiah 5:1–7

We should admire the artistry and rhetorical sophistication of this passage. We are called to imagine a scene in the marketplace, where a strolling player gathers a crowd with the promise of a song whose introduction suggests an enticingly personal element. Ears pricked up, we are taken step by step through an innocent process whose questions draw us in as participants. The case looks clear-cut, so that we are led, all unknowing, to the devastating denouement in verse 7. It reminds us of Nathan's parable, by which David was led to condemn himself for his affair with Bathsheba (2 Samuel 12:1–15). Today's politicians might learn a trick from these ancient sages.

The condemnation, when it comes, is also made memorable by a wordplay. The words for 'justice' and 'bloodshed', and for 'righteousness' and 'a cry', are very similar to each other. Modern attempts to capture the similarities (for example, one scholar's paraphrase: 'He looked for order, what he saw was murder; he looked for right, what he heard was the cry of fright') do not come close to the concise and memorable nature of the original.

Isaiah's literary skill should not overshadow the serious nature of the story to which he has devoted his ploy. We met 'justice and righteousness' in 1:21, where I glossed them as 'social justice'. Isaiah's understanding of the ideal society differs from a modern democracy, as it is strongly hierarchical: God is at the top, and then comes a downward delegation of responsibility for justice to the king, his senior officials and the local officials. Like God, therefore, they should be working tirelessly for the good of those 'beneath' them, not using their privilege for personal gain. The system works only when everyone functions according to this understanding of justice. As in the vineyard, however, despite every advantage of gracious provision, the outcome in Judah has been only wild grapes.

To transfer this judgement to an application in today's world requires an imaginative leap to rival Isaiah's wordplay skills. Like his first listeners, however, we may discover that, as soon as we look for others to condemn in this regard, we find the charge doubling back on ourselves. There is no escape from the song's trap, because we are all guilty sometimes of hypocritical criticism of others.

Optional reading: 2 Samuel 12:1–15; Matthew 21:33–41.

6 A divine conundrum

It is impossible, in just a few words, to do justice to this unusually rich passage. It deserves sustained reflection on what it reveals of the majesty of God and the impact of his holiness.

For today, however, let us focus on his presentation as king, seated among his royal council. When he announces his need of a messenger, Isaiah volunteers (v. 8). The message with which Isaiah is entrusted (vv. 9–10) does not appear elsewhere in his book as having been delivered to the people in so many words. We have to assume (as happens sometimes elsewhere) that this is a 'pseudo-citation'—a summary of what Isaiah believed was the essence of the message he was sent to bring.

There can be no doubt that it is harsh and envisages severe judgement on the people and the land. However, the first half of verse 10 is ambiguous: it is unclear whether it is commanding blessing or hardening. 'Make dull' is literally 'make fat', and everywhere else in the Old Testament fatness is understood as a blessing. Similarly, 'stop' is a word that can mean either 'make heavy' or 'make glorious', while 'shut' is literally 'smear', a rare word that might apply to eye salve. The sentence could be read in two ways, therefore, even though the outcome in the latter half of the verse shows that the negative sense represented in the NRSV is justified.

This observation may help us as we read on in Isaiah and find a puzzling mixture of severe condemnation and judgement on the one hand, and offers of promise and deliverance on the other. The theology is not as simple as saying, 'You have sinned and will therefore be condemned.' Rather, while the reality of sin is squarely faced, God offers a way out, if his gracious invitation is heeded. Sadly, it was not heeded, as we see anticipated in verses 11–13. Paul built on this insight with his reformulation, which the church should still heed: 'Do you not realise that God's kindness is meant to lead you to repentance?' (Romans 2:4).

Optional reading: Psalm 99:1–5; Romans 2:1–11.

Guidelines

There is a startling immediacy about Isaiah's religion. He does not base it at all, as far as we can see, on the standard Old Testament story of the exodus, the ten commandments, and all that. In his vision as recorded in chapter 6, he stands in the direct presence of God the king, and in his teaching elsewhere he finds grounds for criticism in the lack of humility towards God and straightforward justice in the treatment of others. Living under the symbolic shadows of God's presence in the temple in Zion and the rule of his chosen earthly kings, the descendants of David, Isaiah finds direction for living without the need for other embellishments.

His oracles therefore have a freshness that is initially invigorating and liberating. On second thoughts, however, we may find ourselves challenged by the way in which our own religion can get tangled up with concerns that hinder a similar direct encounter with the living and exalted God. So many good things in church life can become all-absorbing, with the resulting danger that we start to forget what they are all there for.

With prayer for complete honesty in our thinking, let us therefore ponder again the grace by which God allows himself to be known to us personally in ways that are suitable to our own individual circumstances, and the response it should evoke of reflecting that grace in practical terms with those whom we meet daily.

1 Immanuel

Isaiah 7:1–17

The context of the prophecy in verse 14 is a threatened invasion of Judah by Israel to the north, in alliance with Aram/Syria. The reason is not stated, although it is usually thought that the allies wanted to draw Judah into an anti-Assyrian coalition and that King Ahaz of Judah was (sensibly) reluctant. Their tactic was not to defeat Judah in battle but to replace Ahaz with a more pliant king of their own choosing (vv. 5–6). This goal is therefore presented as a threat to the ruling Davidic dynasty (see vv. 2, 13).

Isaiah, who was supportive of the family of David, urged Ahaz to resist; the language of verse 4 does not encourage a policy of doing nothing but, rather, is typical of a priestly address to troops before a battle (see Deuteronomy 20:1–4). Faith in the promise that God gave David through Nathan (2 Samuel 7:4–16) should impart confidence (v. 9). To encourage this faith, God offered Ahaz a sign (v. 11), but for some reason Ahaz refused to ask for it. Exasperated by this rejection of God's assurance, Isaiah then gave the 'Immanuel prophecy' (v. 14). The name 'God with us' can indicate either promise or threat, depending on one's stance in faith. While the child is still very young (this is no long-term prediction), the immediate threat will be lifted (vv. 15–16). Equally, God's presence with the unfaithful can lead to judgement (v. 17). Thus, rather as we saw in chapter 6, the rejection of God's positive word inevitably leads to disaster.

Who was Immanuel? This is an age-old debate, and various suggestions have been made—for example, that he was another strangely named son of the prophet, like those in 7:3 and 8:3. It is more likely that he was a royal child, meaning that the future of the dynasty would be secure even if Ahaz's position within it was thereby given notice—again, a combination of hope and threat.

Christians, of course, read the prophecy more fully in the light of Jesus' coming (Matthew 1:23). Without detaching it from its immediate historical context, it may be read very much in the light of its underlying theology—that the Jesus who, as God with us, 'will save his people from their sins' (Matthew 1:21) can also be the stone over which people will stumble if they choose to ignore his gracious invitation (Luke 20:17–18).

Optional reading: 2 Samuel 7:4–16; Matthew 1:18–25.

2 Maher-shalal-hash-baz

Isaiah 8:1–8

This passage returns to Isaiah's own first-person account, which was broken off at the end of chapter 6. There are other links with that chapter too, such as the identity of the audience as 'this people' (v. 6; 6:9–10). It looks as though chapter 7 was inserted to illustrate the outworking of the 'hardening' described in 6:9–10 on the monarchy, and chapter 8 will do the same in relation to the people at large.

The historical setting remains the same as in chapter 7, and the promise in verses 1–4 is again that the invading coalition will not succeed. As with Immanuel, so with this even more strangely named son of the prophet: while he is still very young, the threat will be lifted. Defeat for Israel means deliverance for Judah. Again, we may deduce that the reliably attested prediction of this deliverance, by the writing of the child's name even before he is born, is intended to bolster the faith of the people of Judah in God's protective care of them.

Verses 5–8 tell a different story, however. For reasons that are not stated, the people have chosen to reject God's gracious provision for his people as their king in Zion (this seems to be what is depicted by 'the waters of Shiloah that flow gently'). This rejection applies, immediately, to the promised protection against the current danger, but perhaps speaks more widely of the steps that the people thought they should take in view of the even greater impending threat from Assyria. Whatever the detail, the point is that the rejection of those 'gentle waters' will ultimately lead to the terrifying inundation of the great river (the Euphrates), symbol of the Assyrian ruler and all his military power.

Once again, therefore, we see how the complete disregard of those things that God intends for good can result in catastrophe. 'Keep listening, but do not comprehend' (6:9); would those who later read Isaiah's words ever learn? There are suggestions further on in the book that some did (for example, 29:18; 32:3; 35:5; 42:16; 52:15), but the challenge remains open to all who come after them.

Optional reading: Isaiah 65:1–10; Matthew 23:37–39.

3   Seal the teaching

Isaiah 8:11–20

Verses 11–15 draw together the themes we have been looking at since chapter 6. While Isaiah's teaching has clearly made him very unpopular, God encourages him to keep faith with him rather than be deflected. Verse 13 is the basis for the hymn that says 'Fear him, ye saints, and you will then have nothing else to fear'. That is a good summary of the attitude of people who have genuinely heeded the double-edged warning of 6:9–10. By contrast, as we saw yesterday, 'both houses of Israel'

(v. 14, the two nations of Judah and Israel) have stumbled over the stone that should have been their rock-like security, and so they will fall (vv. 14–15). Israel fell shortly afterwards to the Assyrians, and, although Judah survived that threat by the skin of its teeth, it too eventually fell to the Babylonians.

What should a faithful prophet do in the face of such apparent failure? He is commanded to commit his words to writing (v. 16) and then wait until the judgement is past and the promised brighter future dawns (v. 17). At this early stage in his ministry, it looks as if Isaiah expected the brighter future to arrive within his own lifetime. Later, he came to understand that it would not be realised until a more distant time (see 30:8), but the principle is the same. The first two words of verse 20 should be translated as an exclamation: 'To the teaching and the testimony!' Whether in the face of necromancy (v. 19) or any other deviant practice, the call remains the same; for us, who live so much later, the teaching is included within our written Bible. It remains a secure testimony to God's past faithful treatment of those who kept the faith (as Isaiah did, despite unpopularity), and a warning against deviating from the path of faithfulness that Isaiah so forcefully embodied.

The words 'wait' and 'hope' in verse 17 are used positively in the Old Testament. This is not the waiting of despair, or the expression of 'hope against hope', but a confidence that the promised deliverance will come. Isaiah's disciples (v. 16) and children (v. 18) are emblematic of all those who will join him in this faithful perseverance.

Optional reading: Deuteronomy 13:1–7; 2 Timothy 3:10–17.

4 The messianic king

Isaiah 9:1–7

The last sentence of this passage suggests that it describes a future hope. Although the rest of the passage seems to be describing something that has already happened, this may be a poetic way of describing the certainty of what is expected.

'The people who walked in darkness' (v. 2) are not identified, but the following verses describe liberation from some oppressive power. We may think initially of the Assyrian campaigns that decimated and then obliterated the northern kingdom of Israel (verse 1 refers to those regions, although it is not part of the poem that follows). Equally, the Judeans could have engaged with the passage, as they too suffered seriously, though not quite so catastrophically, under the Assyrians. But the openness of the text means that they could also have applied it when, a century later, the Babylonians brought Judah's independent life to an end. There is also nothing to stop its poetry being taken up by successive generations to give voice to the conviction that no power based solely on military might will be allowed to endure for ever.

Three reasons are given for the joy that will follow, as the word 'for/because' shows at the start of verses 4, 5 and 6. Interestingly, while the first two speak of external deliverance, the third, climactic and longest reason anticipates a major internal change in the country. A new Davidic king has been born. His role, however, is not military but judicial and social. Just as we have seen, in past passages, how Isaiah's indictment is on the abuse of these requirements, so now he anticipates their full realisation.

It is the task rather than the person of the king, therefore, which is of most importance. How the vision should be implemented will vary according to the prevailing circumstances. In independent Judah, the king had authority to implement it directly. Later, when Judah became a colony, the means would necessarily have been different—and would be again, in Jesus' day, when the Son of David could have no political power, given that the country was under Roman occupation (Matthew 4:13–17). The text remains open as long as the role needs fulfilment, however; the challenge for us is to think in turn about how the vision could be implemented in the spirit of Christ in our modern and equally different world.

Optional reading: Psalm 72:1–7; Matthew 4:12–22.

5 The stock of Jesse

Isaiah 10:33—11:9

The last two verses of chapter 10 describe, using the image of forest-felling, how God will bring low the proud and arrogant. Anyone who attempts to rival the 'high and lofty' God (6:1) is bound to fall, according to a persistent theme in Isaiah (see chapter 2, for instance). Here, it is not clear whether the oracle refers to Assyria or to Judah, but with chapter 11 following on directly (11:1 starts, in the original, with the word 'and'), it looks as if it is describing Judah and its leaders.

That, at any rate, gives a good explanation for the image of the new king as a shoot from the stock of Jesse (David's father). The stump of a tree that has been cut down can send up new shoots, so the image suggests a radical new beginning along with an element of continuity. This is not the 'Son of David' of later messianic hope, but a new start after a serious hiatus. Isaiah makes a similarly bold claim using the imagery of building in 28:16–17.

The new king is to be endowed with the spirit of the Lord, which will 'rest' on him (11:2). This form of expression comes only twice elsewhere (Numbers 11:25–26; 2 Kings 2:15), where it is used to designate an assistant or successor. Here, the king is deputising for the divine king, so we might expect the endowment with the spirit to lead to some spiritual fireworks. In fact, his role (vv. 3–5) is, again, the fair administration of justice, as in 9:6–7. Administrators in God's service, members of a group that is often overlooked or even looked down upon, may take encouragement from this depiction of their work's centrality in God's purposes.

Verses 6–9 seem to be added rather abruptly as we move from administration to utopia. The much-loved picture of universal peace derives its force from the combination of powerful hunting animals with young and vulnerable domestic animals. It is this that has led to the more narrowly 'messianic' interpretation of the previous verses, and the image has been the basis for many depictions in Christian art, stretching back as far as we can trace. There is nothing wrong with that, but equally it should not detract from the high value placed on the king's particular role outlined there.

Optional reading: Isaiah 28:14–17; John 10:11–18.

6 Praise for salvation

Isaiah 12

This little hymn of praise serves to round off the first major section of the book in an uplifting way before a new section about foreign nations begins in chapter 13. In tone and in wording, it sounds very like chapters 40—55, where again short hymns are used to divide up the main sections.

Coming here after the chapters that speak both of judgement at the hand of the Assyrians and the prospect of deliverance in the longer term, the use of the hymn is understandably set for the future, 'on that day' (vv. 1, 4). It is a mark of faith, however, to praise God even for promised salvation that has not yet been realised, and that may be the response that is hoped for here.

Like much liturgy, the hymn is suffused with quotations from and allusions to standard psalms, known elsewhere. As just two of several examples, compare verse 2 with Exodus 15:2 and Psalm 118:14, and verse 4 with Psalm 105:1. The heritage of poetic liturgy from our predecessors in the faith is a rich resource, which we should be foolish to undervalue simply because it is not 'new'.

The main theme of the hymn, as articulated in verse 1, is the experience of God's turning from justified anger to comfort and deliverance. The word 'salvation', which comes three times in the next two verses, is the Hebrew word from which the name of Isaiah is derived. Is there an allusion here to the connection between messenger and message? At any event, it serves to remind us that all true faith and Christian experience should be communicated by our lives, not just by our words.

Verse 3 is a bit different. It is the only verse that has no parallels in the Psalms, and the 'you' here is plural, whereas elsewhere it is singular. It is also prose rather than poetry. Could it be a comment, an aside, calling all us readers to draw from the waters of salvation/Isaiah—that is, to meditate on and be strengthened by reflection on the book that we have been reading? In Psalm 1, too, God's word is compared to life-giving water, so the connection may not be as far-fetched as it first appears. At all events, it makes a splendid concluding exhortation to our daily studies.

Optional reading: Psalm 118:1–15; Revelation 5:6–14.

Guidelines

The tone of chapters 7—12 has been generally more positive than that of 1—6, although of course there are exceptions in both halves, so we must be careful not to exaggerate the contrast.

This mixture of positive and negative, darkness and light, is rather confusing; it is sometimes difficult to know quite what to believe. We may, however, reflect on life's experiences in a similar way. We cannot indefinitely escape periods of difficulty or even worse, and, at face value, the way things work out sometimes seems simply unfair. Isaiah has shown us, however, that God's ultimate purposes for his people are always good, even if the path that leads there is seriously uneven.

A particular feature of these chapters has been the so-called 'messianic prophecies' (7:14; 9:6–7; 11:1–9). As we have seen, these passages all make good sense within their immediate historical contexts, but the important point is that they give expression to hopes of a better future ordering of society in all its different forms. They are not just photo-fit elements of a single portrait, which, when completed, looks like Jesus; rather, they articulate what God wants for his world in the light of its present distress. There is no doubt that Jesus embodied to perfection the means whereby those hopes might be realised in his very different circumstances, but the needs of the world are still acute. These prophecies should therefore be read also as a challenge to any who want to be among those who 'imitate Christ' in his form of service.

Is it possible for you to take up the spirit of chapter 12, so that you anticipate praise 'on that day' even if the current circumstances seem to belie it? We sometimes need the broad sweep of Isaiah's vision in order to endure faithfully in current hardships.

FURTHER READING

John Barton, *Isaiah 1—39* (T&T Clark Study Guides), T&T Clark International, 2003.

John Goldingay, *Isaiah* (New International Biblical Commentary), Hendrickson/Paternoster, 2001.

Christopher Seitz, *Isaiah 1—39* (Interpretation), John Knox Press, 1993.

H.G.M. Williamson, *Variations on a Theme: King, Messiah and Servant in the book of Isaiah*, Paternoster, 1988.

Zechariah

Many Old Testament prophets were 'forth-tellers' as much as 'fore-tellers', speaking from the perspective of their own time about events going on around them, explaining the inner dynamic of God's action and what the consequences would be for his people. Where the history of a particular period is well known, it is fairly easy to understand what events and trends the prophets were commenting on; however, there are prophecies that do not easily tie in with what we know of ancient history. There is also material that we call 'apocalyptic'. Some of these passages, whatever their original meaning in the minds of those who uttered or wrote them, are used in the New Testament to highlight Jesus' role as the prophesied Messiah, and are thus treasured by Christians.

The first part of Zechariah (chs. 1—8) includes dates within the text; here we find oracles and visions commenting on what was happening in Jerusalem at that time. In Zechariah 9—14, however, the dates disappear and the utterances are much harder to pin on to known history. They seem often to be reworking earlier prophets' teaching, with a distinctly apocalyptic thrust. Within this mysterious section are passages that the Gospel writers saw as being fulfilled particularly in Jesus' passion.

Those who believe that biblical prophecy and apocalyptic must be fulfilled by precise events have schemas to show which prophecies were fulfilled in the prophets' own days, which in subsequent ancient history, which in Christ's coming, and which are yet to be fulfilled, perhaps at the 'end of the age'. However, this category of 'yet to be fulfilled' prophecy has notoriously given rise to all kinds of expectations at various times, often with huge disillusionment ensuing. It has also fed into hotly disputed theories of the sequence of events at 'the end'.

Another way of looking at the fulfilment of prophecy is through the phrase 'texts that linger, words that explode' (Walter Brueggemann). The prophets' words, for whatever reason they were first uttered, may, in the providence of God, resonate powerfully with events much further on in history, sometimes having repeated relevance. However, 'powerful resonance' does not always mean precise predictive accuracy, as we shall see in the ways in which prophecies from Zechariah 9—14 are embedded in the Gospels.

Quotations are taken from the New Revised Standard Version.

1 The scene is set

Zechariah 1

In around 519BC, Zechariah began to prophesy—first in the eighth month (v. 1), and then, at greater length, in the eleventh month (v. 7). Haggai was prophesying in Jerusalem, too, in the sixth, seventh and ninth months of the same year (Haggai 1:1, 2:1, 10).The two prophets are linked in Ezra 5:1 and 6:14 as companions in encouraging the rebuilding of the temple.

Twenty years earlier, the Persians had conquered the Babylonian empire, instituting a new policy for subject peoples. Those held in exile were encouraged to return home and rebuild their holy places, while remaining under the authority of the Persians. A first party of Judean exiles went from Babylon to Jerusalem, led by Shealtiel, a Davidic prince. However, a series of problems inhibited their temple-building programme—chiefly conflict between those returning and those already in the land (the Samaritans). The latter were descended from the poorer Judeans who had never been transported into exile and had intermarried with foreign settlers whom the Babylonians had planted in the area.

Now, the Persians had conquered Egypt, making Judea much more important strategically as a north–south corridor. This gave them a fresh impulse to re-establish the temple and religious practice of Jerusalem, since the Persians liked to have trusted priestly castes firmly in place in their territories. In this context, Zerubbabel (Shealtiel's son) and Joshua, the hereditary high priest, took up temple-building again, with both imperial and prophetic encouragement.

Today's passage describes the rebuilding of the temple as 'returning' to the Lord after the faithlessness that had originally brought disaster upon the nation (vv. 1–6). It refers to earlier prophets, ignored in their time, in a way that shows that during the years of exile they had acquired quasi-canonical authority. Then comes a vision (vv. 7–21) that includes angels, a feature of Jewish faith that became much heightened in exile. The vision of heavenly beings 'patrolling the earth' (vv. 10–11) reflects the Persian kings' practice of sending out representatives to patrol their dominions.

Zechariah declares that the peace in which the nations dwell is an affront to God and his people, because hostile nations caused the Jews and Israelites to suffer more than was warranted by God's punishment of them (vv. 15, 19–21). Chiefly, however, the message is one of encouragement, of 'gracious and comforting words' (v. 13) regarding the planned rebuilding of the temple.

2 The blessed city

Zechariah 2

Chapter 2 comprises a vision (vv. 1–5) and an oracle (vv. 6–12). Zechariah's vision again involves angels. They provide instructions that clarify the prophecy in 1:16: for the time being (at least), Jerusalem will need no walls, so the reconstruction of the temple takes precedence. (The rebuilding of the walls would take place nearly 70 years later, with Nehemiah, around 445BC.) But the vision is not simply about chronological priorities. It declares that God will be Jerusalem's only necessary defence—'a wall of fire' and 'the glory within it' (v. 5)—blessing it with overflowing prosperity when the temple is re-established.

Commentators have remarked that the image of the firewall may show Persian religious influence, for the Persian ritual capital, Pasargadae, was a city without walls, with fire altars on its perimeter. More interesting for Christians is the way that Zechariah's emphasis on the glory of the Lord in the city's midst parallels Revelation's vision of the new Jerusalem, with 'the glory of God [as] its light' (Revelation 21:23). This theme of God in the midst appears both in the vision and in the oracle (vv. 5, 10, 11), and the oracle links it with the idea of many nations joining themselves to the Lord (compare Revelation 21:24). This theme will be repeated elsewhere in the book of Zechariah, and is also found in Isaiah 56:6–8 (probably the work of a prophet, 'Trito-Isaiah', who prophesied a little later than Zechariah).

The oracle is directed to the Jewish diaspora—the exiles who had not returned to Jerusalem. 'Returns' to the land happened in waves and were never complete: Jews remained settled in Mesopotamia (Iraq) until modern times. The message is urgent: the people *should* return. The image of the singing 'daughter Zion' (v. 10) is old, being found in Isaiah 12:6

and Zephaniah 3:14. The call to return is also found in 'Trito-Isaiah' (for example, Isaiah 60:1–10).

The final utterance of the chapter (v. 13) commands silence before the Lord who is about to act, emphasising that all is due to God's initiative. It repeats the call for awestruck stillness that is found in Habakkuk 2:20 and Zephaniah 1:7 (both earlier prophets), and is a theme of Christian worship today.

3 A messianic age foretold

Zechariah 3:1—5:4

We return to visions, beginning with a picture of the heavenly court (3:1–5). As in the book of Job, Satan is the prosecuting counsel, pinning on Joshua, the hereditary high priest, the guilt of the people's impurity. The 'angel of the Lord' speaks for the Lord himself. He offers a fresh start to the priesthood through Joshua's reclothing, and gives assurance that, in the rebuilt temple, priests will have access to God on the people's behalf. Additionally, a new 'Branch' (of the stock of Jesse, v. 8) will rule, initiating an era of peace (see Isaiah 11:1–9) that is symbolised by the people sitting companionably under each other's vines and fig trees.

The first vision of chapter 4 makes clear who the Davidic 'Branch' is to be: it is Zerubbabel, who is being called to work in cooperation with Joshua on the rebuilding of the temple. The image of a lampstand (4:2) recalls an important feature that belonged in the temple (and the tabernacle, before it), speaking of God's presence. Not only do the flames of the lampstand represent 'the eyes of the Lord' (v. 10) but, remarkably, it seems that Zerubbabel and Joshua together are to be the olive trees from whose oil the flames of the holy lampstand are fed (vv. 12–14). By implication, it is their work that will make possible the powerful presence of the Lord 'in the midst'. But Joshua and Zerubbabel are dependent on the 'spirit of the Lord' (v. 6) to achieve their task; they will achieve an outpouring of his presence on the people because they themselves are 'anointed ones' (v. 14). This is language about a messianic age, but with a dual focus—two anointed ones.

The flying scroll in 5:1–4 suggests the power of the law 'coming home' to the people. Not yet is it to be 'written on their hearts' (as prophesied in

Jeremiah 31:31–34), but it is coming very close, searching out and doing away with evildoers.

4 Balance restored, and a coronation

Zechariah's first vision (1:7–17) involved horses and riders who had returned from patrolling the earth. Chapter 6:1–8 is a related vision, but this one involves charioteers setting off on patrol. The mountains of bronze (v. 1) from between which they issue may be analogous to the metal doors of a temple, since they have just come from the Lord's presence (v. 5).

Commentators cannot agree as to the significance of the different colours of the chariot-horses, nor about why they do not exactly correspond with those in the first vision. It is clear, however, that the chariot is a martial symbol, and when it is identified with storm-wind by Old Testament prophets, the picture is of God attacking and judging (see Isaiah 66:15–16; Jeremiah 4:11–13). So the charioteers of the Lord, the four winds of heaven, are off to bring judgement. Within the vision itself, word comes that the work has been achieved in the north: the nations that had defeated and exiled the Jews have now been punished and the balance of justice restored (compare 1:15, 21).

It is not clear whether any specific event took place, while Zechariah was active, to which this vision might relate, or whether the prophecies in chapters 1 and 6 should be read together as referring to the long time during which Babylon remained unpunished, only to meet its final defeat at the hands of the Persians.

Verses 9–14 are confusing. Why is Zechariah commanded to make a crown for the high priest? Why, apparently, is this priest to be crowned (v. 11), called by the Davidic title 'the Branch' (v. 12; see 3:8; Isaiah 11:1; Jeremiah 33:15) and ascribed royal power (v. 13)? Why is it said that 'he shall build the temple', when 4:9 says this of Zerubbabel? Does today's passage portend the Davidic line's eclipse by the priesthood at this point in history? (Zerubbabel disappears from other annals about this time.) However, some ancient texts read 'crowns' for 'crown' in verses 11 and 14. If we accept this reading and amend verse 11 to 'set *one of them* on the head of the high priest Joshua', we can understand this oracle to be about a double coronation, whereby the Branch (Zerubbabel) and the priest (Joshua) are set side by side in harmony and shared authority, reflecting Zechariah 3:8 and 4:11–14.

The chapter is rounded off with words that link Zechariah's call for more exiles to return with the prospect of success in temple-building. The fulfilment of these prophecies would be the prophet's justification and a sign of the people's obedience (v. 15).

5 A question about fasting

Zechariah 7:1–7; 8:18–19

About two years after Zechariah began prophesying, he spoke again—this time in response to a question. The people of Bethel sent emissaries (7:2) both to the priests and the prophets, asking whether a certain annual fast was really still required. This fast had probably been instituted to commemorate the burning of the temple by Nebuchadnezzar's troops in the fifth month of 587BC (see 2 Kings 25:9; Jeremiah 52:12–13), so maybe they asked the question because the temple was now being rebuilt. Zechariah took the initiative in answering. As recorded in the book we have now, his response was long and complex: a direct answer to the people's question does not appear until 8:18–19.

Some commentators think that Zechariah's prophecies have been edited, with interpolations by an editor (or editors) carrying the distinctive 'Deuteronomistic' theology that informs the book of Deuteronomy and some of the historical books of the Old Testament. Much of the material between the people of Bethel's question and Zechariah's direct answer seems to bear the hallmark of Deuteronomistic thought. Therefore, we shall consider the section between 7:8 and 8:17 separately, tomorrow; today we simply think about the direct answer to the question put in 7:1–3, as found in 8:18–19.

That answer was a joyful and liberating one, for Zechariah told the people that not only the fast they were asking about, but also three other customary fasts, should now be turned on their heads, to become times of celebration. The other customary fasts may also have been associated in people's minds with dire events during the conquest of Jerusalem by the Babylonians—the seventh month with the violent death of Gedaliah (Jeremiah 41:1–2), whom the Babylonians had appointed as regent among the Judeans left in the land after Jerusalem fell; the fourth month with the successful attack on the city (Jeremiah 39:2); and the tenth month with the beginning of the siege in the preceding year (see Jeremiah 39:1).

Zechariah makes it clear that the new celebrations should involve ritual feasting, so they were to be a real turnaround from days of fasting and lamentation. (Nehemiah 8:9–12 gives a lovely picture of such feasting taking place later). But a commitment to truth and peace was still required for God's blessing to be enjoyed (v. 19).

6 Disobedience and restoration

Zechariah 7:4—8:17, 20–23

Today we consider a series of oracles. The first one questions the people's sincerity of heart when they fasted (7:4–7); the second highlights the heart of the law of God and demonstrates how the people's disobedience incurred God's punishment (vv. 8–14). Then comes an oracle of salvation for Jerusalem and 'the remnant' (8:1–8); another develops this theme of salvation by linking it with an exhortation to the people to let 'their hands be strong' in continuing the rebuilding programme (vv. 9–17). In this one it is notable that Haggai and Zechariah seem to be mentioned as prophets whom the people have 'recently been hearing' (v. 9). The last oracle is a vision of many nations coming to worship the Lord in Jerusalem, ending with the significant words of blessing, 'God is with you' (vv. 20–23).

I suggested yesterday that these six oracles (as well as others elsewhere in the book) may be interpolations into Zechariah's own prophecy—interpolations setting the prophet's work within a particular frame of theological interpretation. Certain themes are emphasised—that obedience or disobedience to the law of God is a matter of the heart (7:10, 12a; Deuteronomy 11:18); that the consequence of the nation's disobedience is the kindling of the Lord's anger (7:12b; compare, for example, Deuteronomy 4:25–26); and that this anger has been worked out in history, particularly in the disasters that led to the exile (7:14; Deuteronomy 8:19–20).But there is also a strong theme in this so-called

Deuteronomistic school of thought concerning God's will and ability to restore his people and bless them again, even after punishment (8:1–11; Deuteronomy 32:36–41).

If it is correct that an editor or editors with Deuteronomistic emphases interpolated material among oracles that were original to Zechariah, we can guess that the motives were to underscore the importance of the religion of the heart in the midst of Zechariah's encouragement of the rebuilding of the physical temple, and to set the history of that rebuilding within the sweep of an overall view of history's meaning and direction towards the universal glorification of the Lord in Jerusalem.

Guidelines

You may like to discuss one or more of these questions with a friend who is also using these notes, or you may like to write down some responses in a spiritual journal, even if your conclusions are incomplete and uncertain.

- Zechariah, like Haggai, found a focus of national and religious hope in the project to rebuild the Jerusalem temple. The restored temple did guarantee the continuity of Jewish identity through the tumultuous centuries that followed, but the vision of the temple as the centre of a new messianic kingdom was never wholly fulfilled. In which buildings do we invest our hopes, energy and resources, and what do we expect them to achieve?
- For the Jews, the restoration of their temple was an event of central significance for the whole world; for the Persians, it was just another example of their imperial pacification policy, paralleled by similar restoration projects elsewhere. Can great powers and great religions, with their differing motivations, ever truly work hand in hand? What are the boundary lines that either party cannot overstep without subverting the nature of the other?
- Zechariah must have been disappointed when Zerubbabel did not come to reign as king, and when the exiles did not all flock to return to the land. What resources in scripture help us to come to terms with disappointment, including disappointment with God? What do we learn from the history of the Jews who returned from exile about the nature of the faith and hope we should take from scripture?

- Are we serious enough about both fasting and feasting in 21st-century Christian practice? What is the point of fasting and feasting in biblical thinking?
- Do you associate the keeping of the law with an inward religion of the heart, and of love? In your experience, does concern with the outward 'matter' of religion (buildings, ritual, worship and so on) distract from its inward meaning?

1 The coming king

Zechariah 9

The second part of Zechariah is a mysterious set of writings. Scholars mainly agree that it was appended to the original work of the prophet, although they do not agree how long afterwards, or whether the writings are from one hand or many. The material contains prolific allusions to earlier prophecies, but with an increasingly apocalyptic thrust.

In chapter 9, Christians particularly treasure verses 9 and 10. Matthew 21:5 and John 12:15 cite versions of verse 9 as commentary on Jesus' triumphal entry into Jerusalem, thus shaping its meaning for all who have subsequently seen the verses as linked with Christ's passion. But what did they signify for their original writer, and what would they have meant for subsequent generations of Jews, including those who witnessed Jesus' arrival in Jerusalem?

The command to 'daughter Zion' to rejoice and shout aloud is similar to Zephaniah 3:14–15 and Zechariah 2:10. In those verses, Zion rejoices because of the coming of the Lord *himself* as king into his people's midst. In 9:9, however, it is a human king who comes, riding the animal associated with peace-time. The king's description as 'humble' conjures up other prophecies (for example, Zephaniah 3:12) that describe a specific group of Jews who are favoured by God for their lowly faithfulness.

The original setting of this oracle in Zechariah 9 is between a passage about the pacification of Jerusalem's surrounding enemies (vv. 1–8), which allows the Messiah-king to 'command' peace to the nations (v. 10), and oracles returning to war-like themes (vv. 13–15). In the latter we should notice that it is the Lord who does the fighting, with the people as his weapons (v. 13); it is a war of liberation (v. 11) and salvation (v. 16). The reference to the Greeks in verse 13 may be because they purchased Jews as slaves (see Joel 3:6); however, some commentators see it as evidence that this oracle dates from Alexander the Great's campaigns through the Near East (332–331BC), or that this specific reference was added at that time to words written earlier.

It was the image of an individual human king's arrival, bringing peace for his people, that for centuries fed Jewish messianic expectations. However, its imagery and resonances finally 'exploded' into their Christian meaning, carrying themes of the Lord in the midst, humble lowliness and the bringing of peace, liberation and salvation.

2 Sheep without a shepherd

Zechariah 10

Zechariah 10:2 gives the image of people wandering like sheep without a shepherd. You probably recognise this verse from Mark 6:34 and Matthew 9:36, where we are told that Jesus had 'compassion' on the crowds because (in Matthew's words) 'they were harassed and helpless, like sheep without a shepherd'. Zechariah 10:6 also tells us explicitly of the Lord's compassion for the people, as well as his anger at the leaders who should have been shepherds to them (see, too, Ezekiel 34:1–10).

The author of Zechariah 10, then, was writing in a tradition that imagined the Lord's people as the object of his compassion, like that of a shepherd for his straying sheep. While we do not know his exact historical context, the writer instances a continual tendency among the Hebrews to seek guidance by methods pre-dating monotheism and the law of Moses (today, we might talk about attachment to old superstitions). The consultation of teraphim (small images of household gods) and belief in dreams and divination had all, in earlier days, coexisted with belief in the Lord (see Genesis 31:34; Genesis 40—41), but were condemned by many prophets. Zechariah 10 takes this critical view.

For Christians, who see in Jesus the compassion of a shepherd, the ways in which people may be lost are not specifically described, as they are in Zechariah 10:1–2. This gives us a less restricted message about the 'good shepherd' (John 10:11), the 'shepherd and guardian of [our]souls' (1 Peter 2:25). Ancient beliefs and superstitions not consonant with full trust in Christ continue to be temptations that lead people astray in many cultures; but there are other forces, too, both inward and outward, from which we need his salvation, such as prejudice, the attractions of power and celebrity, and the lure of consumerism.

Zechariah 10:6–12 offers a message of restoration not unlike Second Isaiah's (see Isaiah 43:1–7); it was probably meant to encourage a return to Jerusalem among those who had, so far, elected not to come back from the countries where the Jews had been scattered. There is a natural link between shepherd imagery and the idea of leading people home. For Christians, the idea of being led home takes on a different meaning from the call to return to a physical land and city (see John 14:2).

3 Thirty shekels of silver

Zechariah 11

Chapter 11 begins with warnings of disaster. Then the Lord commands the prophet to shepherd the flock with an attitude of destructive impatience (vv. 8–9) rather than compassion. The naming and breaking of staffs is symbolic prophecy (vv. 7, 10, 14), but it is not clear who annuls the covenant—the prophet or the Lord. God again appoints the prophet as a 'worthless shepherd' (v. 15), only to curse him (v. 17). 'Sheep dealers' are present (vv. 5, 7, 11), who weigh out the prophet's wages—30 shekels of silver (v. 12)—but he throws them into the temple treasury on the Lord's command (v. 13).

Some believe that this mysterious chapter arose from anger about the trading of Jews as slaves by their leaders, but this is surmise. Clearly, though, its warning that the Lord will allow the whole flock's slaughter (v. 6) turns the previous chapter's message about his compassion on its head.

The reference to 30 silver shekels brings to mind Matthew's account of Judas' betrayal and despair (Matthew 27:3–10). Matthew does not explicitly cite Zechariah but fuses elements of this passage with a half-memory of Jeremiah 32:6–9. This illustrates how 'texts that linger, words that explode' from the Old Testament often work in the New Testament.

What is picked up from prophecy is not a detailed foretelling of events, but striking connotations and associations, lingering in the minds of the Gospel writers as they remember, or half-remember, ancient oracles.

In Zechariah, the prophet is told to throw his 30 shekels into the treasury (v. 13). In Matthew, Judas throws down his money in the temple; the chief priests then determine that it cannot go into the treasury, so they buy the potter's field instead. (Intriguingly, an alternative reading of the Zechariah passage speaks of throwing the money 'to the potter'.) So the details carry associations, not exact correspondence.

More important are the connotations spilling from the Zechariah passage—of a heightened crisis for God's people, and of '30 shekels' (the value of the life of a slave: see Exodus 21:32). Zechariah 11:13 refers to the sum sarcastically: 'this lordly price at which I was valued by them'. For Christians, the shocking irony is not about the paltry wage for a shepherd or prophet, but about Christ's life being valued in this way.

4 The one whom they have pierced

Zechariah 12

For the second time in Zechariah part 2, a passage is headed 'An Oracle' (see 9:1). The prophetic language of the book feels increasingly apocalyptic, with repeated use of the phrase 'on that day'. A promise is given, in verses 1–9, of the ultimate triumph of the Lord in Jerusalem, when 'all the nations of the earth shall come together against it' (v. 3). Whereas 9:1–8 specified nations local to the Near East against whom the Lord would defend Jerusalem, here a much more universal sense of enmity (and thus of victory) is being conjured up. But there are signs that, in the prophet's mind, there is tension between Jerusalem and the other towns or clans of Judah, presumably relating to events of his own time (vv. 2, 5, 7). This tension will be resolved by a demonstration of the Lord's special favour to Jerusalem (v. 5), but also by the giving of victory 'to the tents of Judah first, so that… the glory of the inhabitants of Jerusalem may not be exalted over that of Judah' (v. 7).

Prophets of earlier times, such as Zephaniah and Obadiah, had described 'the day of the Lord' as a day of darkness, violence and universal destruction; there was also a longstanding tradition about the Lord fighting in and for Jerusalem (see Isaiah 37:35; Psalm 48:3–8). Zechariah is therefore building on existing traditions but taking them to a new height in his description of the ultimately victorious 'inhabitants of Jerusalem… the feeblest among them… like David, and the house of David… like God, like the angel of the Lord, at their head' (v. 8).

It is the second part of this chapter, verses 10–13, that speaks most powerfully to Christians. Here, the house of David, together with all the Jerusalemites (the royal, priestly and prophetic families), is pictured not in victorious but in penitential mode, mourning 'for the one whom they have pierced' (v. 10). We, like John (John 19:37), naturally see in this enigmatic figure the crucified Jesus. What the reference would have meant to the original author of the prophecy is not clear, although we know that he found members of the Jerusalem 'establishment' guilty of bloodshed—a rather different picture from that of Zerubbabel and Joshua in Zechariah part 1.

5 Stricken shepherd, scattered flock

Zechariah 13

Verses 1–6 continue the theme of penitence. Verse 1 is a promise of God's positive response to the mourning of the house of David and the priests—a fresh start and a new purification. Attention then switches to the continuing idolatry among the Jews; members of the ordinary population will need, and have, a fresh start when the 'names of the idols' are 'cut off from the land' (v. 2). Finally, and perhaps surprisingly in a book bearing a prophet's name, prophets need to be silenced, because they are associated with 'the unclean spirit' (v. 2).

There was a variety of prophets in ancient Israel—the 'professionals' who made their living by it, often in groups; those who felt called as individuals, sometimes against their will; those who saw visions; and those who received messages from God in verbal (oracular) form. By the Persian period, the singing of the Levites in the temple was regarded as a form of prophetic activity (see 1 Chronicles 25:1; 2 Chronicles 20:14; 29:30), and Nehemiah attests to prophets who attempted to intimidate him when he was rebuilding the city walls around 445BC. So it may be that Zechariah 13's uncomplimentary picture of prophets is directed towards some and not all. In a riff on Amos 7:14, we hear that 'professional prophets' will give up the role in favour of agriculture (v. 5). The call to prophets' parents to take draconian measures against them (v. 3) ironically leads to the very kind of bloodshed associated with mourning in the previous chapter.

Verses 7–9 return to the theme of shepherding. 'Strike the shepherd, that the sheep may be scattered' is poignantly quoted by Jesus in Mark 14:27 and Matthew 26:31 as a prophecy of the disciples' flight in Gethsemane. In Zechariah it leads into a prophecy about testing and refining the whole nation through disaster; in the Gospels, the focus is on the testing and refining of a small group in the events of the passion. While the 'worthless shepherd' of Zechariah 11:17 was cursed to be stricken for his desertion of the flock, here the shepherd is, more positively, 'my associate' (v. 7), which is appropriate to the Christian view of Jesus as the shepherd; within the foreknowledge of God, it is the flock which will desert him.

6 The final crisis in Jerusalem

Zechariah 14

The book ends with an apocalyptic crescendo and a final lingering text. Again, the day of the Lord and his defence of Jerusalem are central, but the chapter starts with a prophecy of the Lord gathering 'all the nations' to fight *against* the city, with drastic results. No reason is given for the city's humiliation, nor for the sudden great reversal when the Lord will turn to fight *for* Jerusalem: 'the Lord my God will come, and all the holy ones with him' (v. 5) amid geological upheavals and cosmic phenomena (vv. 4–7, 10), together with waters flowing out to the world from Jerusalem (v. 8; compare Ezekiel 47). In this chapter, the Lord will rule alone (v. 9), not even with a member of the house of David.

The nations that wage war on Jerusalem will be subject to terrible plague and panic, with the result that Jerusalem, once plundered, will become rich with plunder (v. 14). But now comes another reversal: the enemy nations shall themselves survive in remnant, and become the Lord's pilgrim-worshippers at the festival of booths, albeit under threat of drought if they fail in this obligation (vv. 16–19). Jerusalem will become so holy that even the horses' bells will bear the same inscription as the high priest on the Day of Atonement (v. 20; Exodus 28:36), and the bronze pots of the temple—indeed, of the whole city and land—will be sanctified like the silver and gold bowls made for offerings (v. 21). Finally, almost bathetically, comes the concluding text: 'There shall no longer be traders in the house of the Lord of hosts on that day' (v. 21).

Although there are no direct citations from this chapter in the Gospels, these final words resonate strongly for Christians, suggesting that Jesus' cleansing of the temple should be seen at least partly through Zechariah's apocalyptic lens. We may also wish to ponder the oracle about the Mount of Olives: while Zechariah prophesied the Lord's coming there 'and all the holy ones with him' (v. 5), Jesus explicitly rejected the idea of summoning 'legions of angels' when he stood there under arrest (Matthew 26:53). He chose instead to fulfil other prophecies—those of the Suffering Servant, found in the second part of Isaiah (42:1–9; 49:1–7; 50:4–11; 52:13—53:12).

Guidelines

Once again, it may be helpful to discuss some of the following questions with a friend or to jot down your own thoughts, however fragmentary, in a journal and come back to them later.

- Has it been helpful to look in detail at how some of the prophecies of Zechariah 9—13 appear in the Gospels, and to note not only striking correspondences but also places where the events of Christ's life and passion differ from the prophecies? Has your understanding of prophecy changed in any way because of this, or are you more confused about it?
- 'Texts which linger, words that explode' (Walter Brueggemann) suggests that biblical prophecy can take on fresh meaning in differing contexts—the meaning sometimes being jogged in people's imaginations by powerful resonances and associations rather than by direct correspondences. Is this idea an enlightening one, or is it a recipe for simply reading into prophetic writings what we want? What are the dangers here? Conversely, how might the word and Spirit of God be involved in such a process?

- We live in an age that seems almost apocalyptic in terms of the suffering of many people, whether through human cruelty and evil or through 'extreme events' in the world around us. To what extent can you see evidence of God's coming kingdom in all this?
- Zechariah frequently uses the image of shepherding to talk of God's and the prophet's relationship with the people. Can you think of an image that might speak more effectively to members of a modern, non-agrarian society?
- Zechariah is one of several prophets who envisages all the peoples coming to worship the same God in the same place in the final era of peace. Can we, and should we, work towards this goal in our quest for the world's peace? Or does the person of Jesus replace all need for a single geographical place of worship to unify all God's people (see John 4:20–21)?

FURTHER READING

Walter Brueggemann, *Texts that Linger, Words that Explode: Listening to prophetic voices*, Fortress, 2000.

John Eaton, *Mysterious Messages*, SCM, 1997.

David Petersen, *Haggai and Zechariah 1—8*, SCM, 1984.

David Petersen, *Zechariah 9—14 and Malachi*, SCM, 1995.

Paul Redditt, *Introduction to the Prophets*, Eerdmans, 2008.

Revelation 4—22

When we last looked at Revelation, we saw some of the challenges that inhibit our understanding. It is written in a style that is unfamiliar to most of us, although it would have been less strange to John's first readers and hearers. It is saturated with references to the Old Testament, which we know less well than many of those readers did. It also draws on features of John's world of which we are largely unaware. Despite all this, it communicates a vivid and compelling message about what it means to be a faithful witness to Jesus in a world that contests the claims that he makes.

In the coming chapters, we will encounter both the familiar and the unfamiliar—passages that are well known and passages that we find difficult and obscure. We begin with what looks like a reassuring vision of worship 'in heaven', although we will discover some intriguing things in it of which we were unaware. From there we move into the first vision of what is happening in the world, starting with the four horsemen in chapter 6. This movement, from the 'heavenly' to the 'earthly' and back again, is key to our reading. There has already been an oscillation between the two worlds in the opening chapters of the book—although we might not have noticed it yet. John's letter starts off rooted in a particular historical and cultural context—that of the Roman province of Asia in the first century—but looks to a biblical and cosmic vision of Jesus before returning to the realities of daily life. This pattern is repeated and intensified, and implicitly poses the question: what is the relation between the two?

The answer will centre on the person of Jesus, the lamb on the throne looking as though he has been slain. Although he was rich, for our sakes he became poor (2 Corinthians 8:9). Though he was with God, he made his dwelling place among us, that we might see his glory (John 1:14). In his earthly ministry, the kingdom of heaven came among us (Luke 11:20). Now, seated at the right hand of the one on the throne, he shares God's praise and, through his prayer as our great high priest, continues to hold earth and heaven together—until the day when they are reunited, as the new Jerusalem comes down and God is with his people for ever more.

1 When two (or three) worlds collide

Revelation 4—5

As we travel with John through a door into a heavenly throne room (4:1–2), we might feel overwhelmed by the sights, sounds and smells of this extraordinary world of worship. Yet, as our senses become accustomed to what is around us, we can gradually make out two other worlds that have come together in this portrait of spiritual reality.

The first is the biblical world of Old Testament worship. The temple trumpet summons John, and he is lifted by the Spirit to the throne as Ezekiel was; he sees jewels from Eden and Noah's rainbow; he hears Sinai's thunder and lightning, which signal the presence of the Almighty, and is surrounded by Zechariah's seven torches and the sea of glass from Solomon's temple. This is an encounter with the God who made the world, who longs to see its restoration, and who travelled the long journey of redemption with his people.

This reality is intertwined with another—the world of the Roman empire and the worship of its emperor. Here, city elders dress in white and bow down to their august ruler, casting their crowns and hailing him with choruses. But, says John, it is the Creator God who deserves this honour, and not any human ruler (vv. 9–11). Any human who claims to be the source of peace and prosperity is usurping God's rightful praise; all such praise rightly belongs to him.

Into these two worlds, John then blends a third—the new thing that God has done in Jesus. It is Jesus who has fulfilled the purposes of God for his people, so it is he who can unlock the secrets of God's dealings with the world (5:5). It is Jesus who is able to release God's Spirit into the world (v. 6) and enable God's people to become all they were intended to be—exercising a priestly role to the whole world, bringing God to the nations and the nations to God (vv. 9–10). Jesus has not only laid down his life for others; he has also taken it back from God, so the Lamb who was slaughtered now lives again. Every knee bows and every tongue confesses his praise, and his glory and his name are indistinguishable from the one on the throne (vv. 11–13; compare Philippians 2:10–11).

2 The suffering… and the glory?

The scroll that has been given to the Lamb looks very much like a 'last will and testament', and, as its seals are broken, we get a first glimpse of God's will for his world. We turn our gaze from the dazzling and ordered vision of the throne, and are confronted with the dark and chaotic realities of life on earth.

As always, John reaches for biblical ideas to depict the scene, adapting the four horses from Zechariah 1. There, they signified a false peace; here, they signify global calamity. This is not some future apocalypse that God is waiting to unleash on the world, but a depiction of the world as it is—a world plagued by false religion (the white horse: note the bow of Apollo that the rider carries), war (red), famine (black) and death (pale green). If you not convinced by this depiction, just open a newspaper or watch the television news!

As God's purposes unfold with the opening of the fifth seal, we see God's people suffering persecution but, nevertheless, enjoying God's protection and safe-keeping under the altar (v. 9). We have already met the theme of outward oppression and inner protection, and it will be repeated again in more detail. The saints who have suffered don't appear to be followers of the Lamb; unlike John, the word of God they held to was 'testimony', but not yet 'testimony of Jesus' (compare 1:9). In fact, they are waiting for their other 'brothers and sisters' (v. 11) to be added to their number.

With the sixth seal comes the resolution of both the violence of the world and the persecution of the saints: God comes in judgement (vv. 12–17). John uses images from Isaiah 34:4 (the sky rolled like a scroll) as well as from Joel 2:31 (the darkened sun and the moon turned to blood), relating to the Day of the Lord and the end of the age. This imagery is used by Jesus (Matthew 24) and at Pentecost by Peter (Acts 2). In Jesus' death and resurrection and the giving of the Spirit, the new age has broken in, although the final judgement on 'this' age is still to come. So Revelation 6 paints a broad-brush history of the world in biblical terms. Having turned from God, the world suffers pain and confusion, rejecting the testimony of God's people and hurtling towards judgement.

3 God's first answer

Revelation 7

We have seen a first sketch of what the world is like in chapter 6, which has already raised the question, 'How long, O Lord?' (6:10). What can God do with a world that, created in love, has gone so badly wrong? Chapter 7, coming as an interlude before the final seal is opened in 8:1, offers the first sketch of an answer.

Verses 1–3 echo Ezekiel's account of God's people being sealed to protect them from the calamities and judgement that the world experiences (Ezekiel 9). Note that John hears the number of those who are sealed: they are being counted out, tribe by tribe, just as Moses counted the people in the desert and David counted the people in the land. In both of these cases, the purpose was to assess the fighting strength of the people, since every man would be expected to fight. So here we have a disciplined ordering of God's people, ready for spiritual warfare. The list of tribes here is different from any Old Testament list and omits the tribe of Dan, who were guilty of idol worship. Our readiness for spiritual conflict is connected to our worship of God.

John then looks to see those he has been hearing about (v. 9). As previously ('I turned to see the voice', 1:12), the things that John sees and hears interpret each other. Those who are counted and ready for battle are, in fact, uncountable; the twelve tribes of Israel are now composed of people from 'every nation, tribe, people and language' as a result of the ransom of the Lamb. God's people are no longer saved 'out of *all* nations' (Exodus 19:5), as people separated from others by clear boundaries, but are saved 'out of *every* nation', as a new community that can be found distributed in every part of the world.

These people are characterised by two apparently conflicting features. The first is that, like John himself and the souls under the throne, they suffer, coming through the 'great ordeal' which is the experience of all who worship the Lamb who was slain (v. 14). The second is that, despite this, they are caught up in praise of God and the Lamb. Like John, they have also already experienced the kingdom, and in their praise they give us a foretaste of the splendours of the city we will see in chapter 21.

4 Heaven, earth... and hell?

Turning from the interlude of chapter 7, we are confronted with an unrelenting litany of evil and suffering on earth. And yet, even in this, there is reason for hope.

We can recognise the world depicted here. There are strong echoes of the plagues sent on Egypt as a warning to recognise God and let his people go, but there are echoes, too, of real events in the world of John's readers. For example, the blazing mountain (8:8) looks very much like the erupting Mount Vesuvius in AD79. Then, moving down the centuries, how could those who witnessed the slaughter perpetrated by Genghis Khan, or the Black Death, or the Thirty Years' War, or the environmental disasters in the Soviet Union, not see some echo of their own world in these verses? We do not have to wait either for a future catastrophic judgement or for a magical escape route before we see God taking action to engage with our reality; it is this messy and violent world that God both loves and redeems—and that is one reason for hope.

A second reason is that these chapters continue to have a connection with the vision of heaven in chapters 4 and 5. In some strange way, the events on earth are influenced by the 'prayers of all the saints' before the throne (8:3). Also, though not immune from suffering, those with 'the seal of God on their foreheads' (9:4) experience God's protection, promised in chapter 7.

The third reason for hope is that this is not the final word on God's will for his world. John has presented God as almighty, the one who sees all and is sovereign over all, but he is reticent about portraying these events as being directed by God. Although the angels stand before the throne, they have only an oblique role in what is happening. The earth is 'burned' (8:7), a mountain is 'thrown' (v. 8), and the sun, moon and stars are 'struck' (v. 12). Yet this chaos is still under the ordering of God in the numbering of the trumpet blasts—even if that ordering is strained to its limits. The outcome is not yet the repentance of the people (9:21)—that will have to wait until God's decisive intervention through his faithful witnesses (11:13)—but their repentance is what God still longs for.

5 The bittersweet message

Revelation 10—11

As we had between the sixth and seventh seals, so we have an interlude between the sixth and seventh trumpets. In both cases, we are offered a vision of God's people as the answer to the question of how God will bring this broken world back to him.

After the dark storms of the previous chapters, there comes a break in the clouds and a ray of light shines through. A 'mighty angel' appears (10:1), wrapped in the resulting rainbow—a visual reminder of God's commitment to his world, as the creator, not the destroyer. This reminder is reinforced by the passing over of another series of judgements, the seven thunders, so that the fulfilment of God's plans for redemption can be announced 'without delay' (10:6). The angel swears solemnly, in the name of God the creator, reminding us of the heavenly praise in chapter 4.

Now that the seals on the scroll have been broken, the scroll itself is open. Like Ezekiel before him, John symbolically eats it: he takes the message in so that he can then speak it out. Since those redeemed will come from 'every tribe, language, people and nation' (5:9; 7:9), the message must be proclaimed to them all (10:11).

The message is sweet because it is 'good news' for the servants of God (the verb 'proclaimed' in 10:7 is *euangelizomia*, from which we get 'evangelism'), but it is bitter because it heralds both their own suffering and judgement on those who do not receive the message.

John spells out what this means in two images of the people of God. First, they are the 'temple of God', just as those who keep faith will be 'pillars' in the temple (3:12) and each community is a 'lampstand' in the sanctuary (1:12). Once again, they appear to suffer as the outer courts are 'trampled' (11:2), but the inner sanctuary is kept under God's protection. Second, they are 'two witnesses' who exercise the ministry of Joshua and Zerubbabel (see Zechariah 3—4) and the ministries of Elijah (who shut the sky) and Moses (who struck the water and earth). Like Jesus, the archetypal faithful witness, they appear to have been defeated and killed by their enemies, but God raises them to life once more. As victory is proclaimed and God's purposes are fulfilled, his 'temple in heaven' is opened (11:19) to reveal the secret of their success.

6 The heart of the matter

Revelation 12

We now reach the clearest revelation of the message of the book—although, for many of us, it still remains cloaked in mystery. As elsewhere, that cloak is woven from two threads: the story of the Old Testament and the first-century world of John's readers.

The Old Testament provides us with the characters for the story. The woman 'clothed with the sun' is the people of God, crying out in pain as they long to be 'delivered' from birthpangs. They are awaiting the age that is to come (Isaiah 66:7; Micah 4:10; 5:3), brought in by God's anointed one. The 'male child' is the promised king who will 'rule the nations with a rod of iron' (Psalm 2:9). The great dragon is that primeval opponent of God who has been testing God's people down the centuries.

Like a master political cartoonist, John combines these characters with a story from a very different source—one that is unfamiliar to most of us but would have been well known to all his first hearers. It is the story of the conflict between the chaos monster Python and the hero Apollo, with his sister Artemis. Python waits before Apollo's mother, Leto, to consume her newborn child before he can come to maturity. But both children and mother are snatched away to safety, carried on the wings of an eagle and protected by water, until Apollo uses his bow and arrows to kill Python.

This story was well known as imperial propaganda. The emperor and his power were like the hero Apollo, slaying the chaos monster of war and want by bringing *Pax Romana*, the peace and prosperity of the Roman empire. But John turns the story inside out. It is Jesus, the promised deliverer, who is the hero and victor, and his triumph comes not through political or military might but by his dying and rising again ('by the blood of the Lamb', v. 11). Despite all appearances to the contrary, it is the followers of the Lamb who will be kept safe and will share in the final victory of the Lamb. Those who trust in the emperor for salvation are unwittingly in allegiance with the power that has opposed God from the very beginning, the one who was defeated on the cross and will ultimately be destroyed.

In the contest for our allegiance, the stakes have never been higher.

Guidelines

One of the most profound questions anyone can ask us is 'What do you see?' (Amos 7:8; 8:2). What do we see when we look at the world around us, and when we look to God?

These chapters challenge us to look carefully. They invite us to see the world as created by God and loved by him. Even though it has turned from him, he is determined to hold out the possibility of repentance and redemption. We are also challenged to see the world as it is, in all its chaos and pain. The constant stream of images on our television news might be in danger of giving us 'compassion fatigue', but Revelation calls us to keep on looking and not to turn our gaze away. In all its pain, there is still hope for our world in the suffering and risen Jesus.

These chapters also challenge us to look again at God. In the 'seven spirits of God sent out into all the earth' (5:6), God is neither absent from his world nor indifferent to it. Revelation aims to tread a fine line between the question of God's sovereignty and his love: if God is in control and loves the world, why is there so much suffering? What it makes clear is that God is creator, not destroyer, and it offers glimpses into the future where 'the kingdom of the world has become the kingdom of our Lord and of his Messiah' (11:15), where 'God will wipe away every tear from their eyes' (7:17).

Lastly, these chapters challenge us to look at who we are as the people of God. The cry goes up, 'How long, O Lord? What will you do about the state of the world?' And the answer comes back repeatedly: God will form a people to be faithful witnesses to his truth. As Bill Hybels often expresses it, the local church is the hope of the world. As lights shining in the darkness, we are here to point people to the light of the world. This is God's plan of redemption for the world; there is no Plan B! God's victory and truth are made known both by Jesus' sacrificial death ('the blood of the Lamb') and in our faithful expression of it in our lives ('the word of their testimony') (12:11).

1 Decision time

Revelation 13

The transition from chapter 12 to 13 follows the consistent pattern that we have seen unfolding in the book. The focus 'in heaven' (12:1) now switches to earth and what is happening there. As previously, the 'heavenly' reality is that God's people are kept safe and nourished (12:14), even though the earthly experience is that they appear to have been conquered (13:7).

Through his death and resurrection Jesus has won the victory, but that victory is not unopposed, and now the cosmic conflict between God and the devil unfolds. In every aspect of this conflict, the devil offers a distorted imitation of God's own action. As God shares his power with the Lamb and the 'seven spirits', so the devil shares his power with the two beasts (v. 2). As the Lamb appeared to have been slain, so the beast from the sea appears to have received a mortal wound (v. 3). The angel Michael, by his very name, reminds us of the worship of God: 'Who [Mi-] is like [-cha-] God [-el]?' (12:7). Now this cry of amazement expresses worship of the beast (13:4). As the Lamb redeems people 'from every tribe, language, people and nation' (5:9), so these are the very people seduced by the power of the beast (13:7).

The two witnesses in chapter 11 performed signs, including calling down fire on earth (v. 5), and the second beast performs similar signs (13:13). The followers of the Lamb are marked with a seal (7:4), and so the followers of the beast receive its mark, which is a number (13:17). The number 666 is designed not to conceal but to reveal its identity; once again, our cultural distance makes it puzzling. John's first readers would have recognised the name of Nero Caesar (written in Greek, but using Hebrew letters) behind this number; thus, if you want to know the true spirit of the empire, simply look at the actions of Nero.

For John, this is just the latest manifestation of human hubris, dressed in imperial clothing. With its ten horns, its blasphemy and its war on the saints, the beast looks like the last of Daniel's four empire-beasts (Daniel 7:1–8), but, as a leopard-bear-lion, it actually shares features of all four.

The decision on loyalty—to divine kingdom or human empire—is one that confronts every generation, including ours. Neutrality is not an option.

2 Salvation and judgement

Revelation 14—15

Another sudden change of view offers a dramatic contrast to the perspective of chapter 13. Though apparently trampled by the beast, the saints (like the 144,000 from 7:4–8) are nevertheless kept safe on Mount Zion, the place of God's presence and praise. The protective seal (7:3) turns out to be the name of the Lamb, now indistinguishable from the name of God (14:1; compare Philippians 2:9), just as the mark of the beast is its name. The character of the worshipped shapes the life of the worshipper.

The description of these men as 'virgins' (v. 4) cannot be literal, since the word 'virgin' is feminine, and the other symbol of God's people, the woman clothed with the sun, has many offspring (12:17). Once more, the vision anticipates the ultimate end: these believers are the 'firstfruits' of the harvest to come (compare Romans 8:23).

If final salvation is anticipated, so is final judgement, with the first mention of 'Babylon' as a metaphor for Rome—both empires having destroyed Jerusalem. This judgement will be comprehensive: the word 'sickle' comes seven times in chapter 14, indicating completeness.

These troubling images of God's wrath are ameliorated by three vital features of the text. First, the basis for celebration is not that God's judgement has *come*, but that God's judgements are *true* (15:3). God's 'wrath' is always a noun, never a verb; it represents God's steadfast opposition to all that is evil, and is shown by God's allowing people to reap the consequences of what they have sown (compare Romans 1:18–32, where God's wrath is being revealed in his 'handing over' of the offenders).

Second, although the judgement is God's, he is always one step removed from its execution. Just as the voices of the living creatures called forth the four horsemen in chapter 6, and angels blew trumpets in chapter 8, so here another angel swings the sickle that exacts the judgement of the Son of Man (14:19).

Third and most strikingly, the 'song of Moses' sung by the saved

(15:3–4) has been rewritten by the Lamb who was slain. The first song of Moses, in Exodus 15, celebrated God's victory and rejoiced in the destruction of God's enemies. But in this 'new' song, the victory of God is found not in the destruction of his enemies but in their redemption.

3 Just judgement

The seven bowls rehearse much of what we have seen before in the seven seals and the seven trumpets, though more briefly and with a slight change of emphasis. The plagues bring a stronger echo of the ten plagues of Egypt, with the water turning to blood, the sores and the frogs.

Now that God's plans have been made clear and the invitation to follow the Lamb has been held out, two themes emerge. The first is the repeated, explicit invitation to 'repent' (16:9, 11). God's desire is for redemption, not destruction. The second theme is the justice of God; harsh though the plagues sound, in John's vision all the players are convinced that God's judgements are 'true and just' (16:7). If we find this claim difficult to swallow, perhaps we need to spend time with God, as Abraham did before the destruction of Sodom and Gomorrah, asking, 'Will not the Judge of all the earth do right?' (Genesis 18:25).

The climax of judgement is marked by conflict, chaos and the collapse of the known order of things. The focus of conflict is symbolically located at Har Megiddo (v. 16), on the south side of the plain of Jezreel, between the hills of Galilee and the ridge of Mount Carmel. Many times in history, this was the place where the fate of God's people was decided.

Chapters 17 and 18 are inserted into this last moment of judgement, zooming in to give us a close-up of what God's judgement will mean for the centre of imperial power. As we have seen before (in the mention of Jezebel in 2:20–22 and the saints as virgins in 14:4), sexual infidelity is used as a metaphor for the worship of other gods. In our contemporary context, this imagery might present us with some ethical concerns, but it continues a long tradition of biblical symbolism, not least in the lived-out parable of Hosea and Gomer. The woman is depicted as a wealthy courtesan, illustrating the financial gain that has come for Rome as the centre of religious, political and military power (it 'rules over the kings of the earth', 17:18). The numbering of the kings (vv. 10, 12) is not there to tell us when John was writing, but to confirm that 'their time is short' and that ultimate victory belongs to the Lamb and those who stay faithful to him (v. 14).

4   Investing in the future

Revelation 18

Most of this chapter takes the form of a poetic song, and in English versions the lines are indented to show this, but the song conveys contrasting messages.

At the beginning and end are songs of praise and celebration: 'Fallen! Fallen is Babylon the Great!... Rejoice over her, O heaven, you saints and apostles and prophets!' (18:2, 20). The language of judgement here echoes the language of the spiritual victory won by the 'male child' over the dragon in chapter 12. Just as there was 'no more room found' for the dragon in heaven (12:8), so now the city of Babylon, with all the sights and sounds of prosperity, 'will be found no more' (18:21). The reason for the rejoicing is not that all this human creativity, craftsmanship and trade has been lost, but that the cost of it has been so high. Not only has it involved the persecution of the saints; it has included the death of 'all who have been slaughtered on the earth' (v. 24).

Within the celebration is a contrasting threefold lament (vv. 9–19). The first part comes from the 'kings of the earth' who have benefited from 'Babylon' even as they have been ruled over by her (v. 9; 17:18). Yet their lament appears to be more for their loss than for hers; not wanting to be drawn into the judgement themselves, they 'stand far off' (v. 10). In the second lament, by the 'merchants of the earth', the self-interest is even more explicit. Also standing 'far off' (v. 15), they mourn their own loss: 'no one buys their cargoes any more' (v. 11). The third lament comes from those who manned the ships. They too stand far off and mourn the loss of their opportunity to grow wealthy. In this empire, worship and wealth have gone hand in hand, and (as Paul discovered from the silversmiths in Ephesus, Acts 19:24–27), woe betide anyone who stands in the way of it!

For John's readers, both the praise and the lament still lie in the future, but knowing the destiny of the great city creates an ethical imperative.

So between the praise and the lament comes the challenge to decide (vv. 4–8). Like God's people in exile 600 years before (Isaiah 52:11), their future lies in trusting God, not investing in the ways of Babylon.

5 Visions of the end

Revelation 19—20

The celebration that opens chapter 19 brings together the different elements of praise we have already encountered, and introduces some new ones to prepare us for the grand finale. We hear from the 'great multitude' (see 7:9), who offer the opening anthem, and from the 24 elders and four living creatures (4:4–8), who respond with their own 'Hallelujah!' A further response comes from the 'voice from the throne' who announced 'It is done!' in 16:17, and there is a final, antiphonal response from the swelling multitude. The praise has moved from celebrating God as creator, to celebrating the Lamb as redeemer, through celebrating their victory over evil, and finally (introducing the idea of bride and bridegroom) the reconciliation of all creation. This is no new prophetic message, different from the good news in the rest of the New Testament, but simply a faithful testimony to all that Jesus has done (19:10).

We should by now have realised that Revelation is not offering a linear chronology of 'end times' events, but a cyclical exploration of how the world is, what God has done about it, and how it will all end. What now follows is a series of seven visions, each introduced by 'Then I saw…' (19:11, 17, 19; 20:1, 4, 11; 21:1). These are not a sequence of events so much as different perspectives on what 'the end' will look like and achieve, drawing on different sets of images.

Jesus' Lordship over the nations will be realised; having been 'ruler of the kings of the earth' (1:5) *de jure*, he now becomes their king and Lord *de facto*. The army that was counted out in chapter 7 now joins the battle (19:14) but, despite the gory imagery, it is important to notice what kind of battle this is. The king's weapon is not a real sword, but something that comes from his mouth—the word of truth (19:15)—and the uniform of the army is not armour, but their 'righteous deeds' (v. 8), which are theirs because of the death of Jesus (7:14).

The millennium (20:4) is based on a rabbinical idea that the world has seven ages of 1000 years, and that the Messiah will usher in an eighth. The saints who have been oppressed on earth will be vindicated *on earth*. The victory will come not through human effort but by God's action ('fire from heaven', 20:9), and God's just judgement will be complete (20:11–15).

6 The new Jerusalem

Revelation 21—22

The final vision is an extraordinary kaleidoscope of hope fulfilled. It draws from almost every strand of the Old Testament, telling us again and again that the Lamb who has been slain answers every hope of the people of God, now drawn from every nation in the world. Jesus really is the 'yes' to all God's promises (2 Corinthians 1:20). The new thing that God has done in Jesus is the fullest expression of what he has always been doing; the gates of the city have the names of the twelve tribes of Israel, and the foundations have the names of the twelve apostles, the leaders of the renewed Israel.

The new Jerusalem comes down from a renewed heaven to a renewed earth; our destiny is not to be disembodied with God in a spiritual heaven, but to be raised to bodily resurrection life, just as Jesus was. For the first time, the one on the throne speaks directly, and it is to announce his tender and compassionate presence with his people for ever. The 'city' is not so much a place for his people to dwell as the people themselves; the new Jerusalem is the bride of the Lamb, and God is present both in and with his people. They have been perfected by him so that they present a vision of unimaginable beauty and radiance. As the dwelling place of God, this redeemed people has become the temple—which is why there is no need for a temple in the city (21:22; compare 1 Corinthians 3:16; 1 Peter 2:5). The city is a perfect cube (21:16), representing not just the temple but the Holy of Holies, the place of the *shekinah* presence of God himself.

From all that has gone before, and the sharp division of humanity that John has drawn in setting out his challenge of decision, we might expect that the invitation to enter this city would be limited and exclusive. In some ways it is: there is no room for the selfishness and imperfection of sin (21:8). Yet there are also surprising elements of a universal vision of redemption. The light of God and the Lamb is not just for God's people in a narrow sense: 'the nations will walk by its light, and the kings of the earth' (whom we might expect to be excluded) 'will bring their splendour into it' (21:24).

Guidelines

You might be feeling a little giddy at the end of our whistle-stop tour of the most exciting, influential, complex and engaging book of the New Testament, but you might also be feeling disturbed by the apparent violence of some of the imagery, especially in the last few chapters. There is much debate about what this means for our appreciation of the book, and there are no simple answers to help us overcome our cultural distance from the text. But we do need to bear in mind some key issues as we continue to reflect.

First, the God of the book of Revelation is the same God who loved us and gave himself for us, who was in Christ, reconciling the world to himself. The text of Revelation makes this claim repeatedly.

Second, one of the key aims of the book is to confirm and challenge our faith. The drama of its images, the rapid movement from one scene to the next, and the sharp contrast in the destinies of the main characters all communicate the supreme importance of 'seeking first the kingdom of God and what he requires' (Matthew 6:33). If we invest our time, energy, trust and loyalty in things that are ultimately contrary to God's purposes, these things will be lost and our investment will be without return.

This calls for both decision and action. Unlike the words of Daniel (Daniel 12:4), the words of this book are *not* to be 'sealed up' (22:10). Rather than standing still, waiting for something to happen, we are to grasp this hope and live it out in our everyday lives.

The final note of the book is the generosity of God's invitation to all. Down the centuries, some readers of this text have used it to confirm them in their prejudices, to limit God's welcome and close the door on people who are 'not like them', but Revelation will not allow us to do this. The gates of the city will never be shut. 'Let the one who is thirsty come; and let the one who wishes take the free gift of the water of life' (22:17). If Revelation does not make us more committed in our discipleship *and* more generous in our invitation to others, it has not done its work.

Ezra

The curious book of Ezra poses readers with a number of problems. Ezra himself does not appear until halfway through the book that bears his name, after which much is composed from his personal memoirs. Chapters 1—6 refer to a much earlier time (although some scholars date it differently). Ezra's work overlaps with Nehemiah's, but Ezra doesn't mention him (the Nehemiah mentioned in Ezra 2:2 can't be the author of the book of Nehemiah). Nehemiah chapters 8 and 12 mention Ezra but don't present his role quite as we might expect. How do these two books fit together, and how do they fit with 1 and 2 Chronicles? In some respects they seem to complete the story started there, which was suspended by the exile, but in other respects their emphases are different. And how does Ezra dovetail with the ministry of Haggai and Zechariah? He mentions them (5:1; 6:14) but doesn't communicate exactly the same message as they do. The 'further reading' listed at the end of the notes will be helpful on these matters.

Ezra and Nehemiah both document what happened when successive groups of Jews returned to their homeland after the exile. There are three parts to the story. First, Ezra records the initial group's return and their re-building of the temple (chs. 1—6), during the period 538–516BC. Then, Ezra narrates his own return with a second group, which took place in 458BC, and the re-establishment of the law (chs. 7—10). Finally, Nehemiah tells of a later return, in 446/5BC, when the walls of Jerusalem were rebuilt.

The focus of these books is twofold. First, they are a testimony to the remarkable providence of God in using the political powers of the Persian world to achieve his purposes and support his people in their return and renewal, in spite of opposition and conflict. Second, they stress the importance of the temple, the Torah (the law, probably the Pentateuch) and the city wall in giving this returning remnant their unique identity as God's elect people. Ezra deals with the temple and the Torah; the wall is left to Nehemiah, later.

Whatever the historical problems with the text, the spiritual lessons we can draw from it are clear and challenging, not least in its teaching about separation.

Quotations are taken from the New International Version of the Bible.

1 The first return

Ezra 1

Momentous changes took place when Cyrus assumed power and the Persian empire replaced that of Babylon. He reversed Babylon's policy of deportation and issued an edict permitting exiles to return home, taking with them the treasures that had been purloined from their temples and storehouses. His edict of 538BC is recorded on a clay cylinder now exhibited in the British Museum. The policy benefited many peoples, among them the Jews. So a group of at least 42,360 (2:64) returned home, taking over 5000 precious objects with them (1:9–11).

From Cyrus' viewpoint, this was wise foreign policy, but Israel could detect God's hand in it. To them, it was evidence of God's sovereignty. He truly was 'King of kings' and the change really took place because God 'moved the heart of Cyrus' (v. 1). In his proclamation of freedom, Cyrus refers to 'the Lord, the God of heaven' (v. 2). He doesn't say this as a result of conversion or personal conviction, however; sadly, it's most likely merely the language of diplomacy. Israel saw more than the providence of God in this move: it was a witness to God's faithfulness. God had pledged through Jeremiah (Jeremiah 25:12; 29:10) that the exile would last 70 years and then Babylon would be overthrown, and so it was. God was keeping his promise—but he was doing so with one slight change. The return was happening after only 50 years rather than 70. Such is God's grace in cutting short the disciplining of his people.

It wasn't only Cyrus' heart that had to be 'moved'. A corresponding work of God in the hearts of the exiles was needed if Cyrus' policy was to work. We might wonder if God sometimes gives his people opportunities through 'the powers that be', which they do not exploit because their own hearts are fixed and settled rather than open and adventurous.

While acknowledging that some people had never been deported and were 'survivors' (v. 4) in the land, the story is presented as a new exodus. The wealth given to the returning exiles by the Babylonians echoes the way Egyptians gave silver and gold to the Israelites in Exodus 12:35–36. This new exodus heralded a new start for God's people, back in their land, where they could faithfully serve him as people of the covenant.

2 Rebuilding

The exiles who returned set about re-establishing their religious rituals. Every sentence of the account of their doing so is full of significance.

The first thing they did was to 'build the altar' and revive the daily, annual and freewill offerings (v. 2). They didn't wait until the temple itself was rebuilt; they established priorities. The fact that they couldn't do everything didn't stop them from starting somewhere (v. 7). The report draws attention to their unity (v. 1), the good leadership they enjoyed (v. 2) and the courage they displayed (v. 3). The double emphasis on the law (vv. 2, 4) shows that their real concern was to obey it. From the start, the resettled community was shaped by the Mosaic law, even if subsequently they did not live as much in accordance with it as they might have thought (chs. 9—10; Nehemiah 13:23–31). They did all this in a festival month (Leviticus 23:23–43), starting with the Festival of Tabernacles, a further reminder of the exodus and an appropriate way to celebrate the new exodus they were experiencing themselves.

After the altar, they set about rebuilding the temple itself (vv. 7–13). Much of the report, including mention of the contributions from Tyre and Sidon, is designed to provoke memories of building Solomon's temple (2 Chronicles 2:8–16). The work was well organised, with Levites as young as 20 doing the work under careful supervision (vv. 8–9). The difficulty was that, even at the foundation-laying stage, it was obvious that this new temple wasn't going to be a patch on Solomon's. So when they stopped to praise God for their progress, while many rejoiced, 'many of the older priests and Levites' who remembered Solomon's temple 'wept aloud' (vv. 11–12).

The prophet Haggai confronted their disappointment head-on (Haggai 2:1–9), assuring them that God was with them and would reveal his glory even more through their modest temple than he had through Solomon's magnificent edifice. It was no longer Solomon's day; the situation was altogether different. But God wasn't limited to working only as he had done in the past or only through one type of building; nor was he restricted by different economic and political circumstances. The Lord is good and his covenant love endures, and that was what counted (v. 11).

3 Opposition

Ezra 4 is both a sandwich and a signpost. Let me explain! The rebuilding of the temple, begun in 538BC, immediately provoked opposition from 'the enemies' around them, who set out to prevent its progress. That opposition is reported in verses 1–5 and picked up again in verse 24— hence the sandwich. Verse 24 tells us that as a result of the opposition, 'the work came to a standstill' until 520BC. This prepares us for what follows in chapters 5 and 6.

Between verses 5 and 24 (as the 'meat in the sandwich'), Ezra looks forward to a much later time when they encountered further opposition, during the reigns of Xerxes (also known as Ahasuerus, 486–465BC) and Artaxeres (465–424BC). This is a signpost, pointing to the future. McConville (*Ezra, Nehemiah and Esther*, p. 25) calls it a 'flash-forward' as opposed to a 'flashback'. These later events are detailed more fully in Ezra 7 to Nehemiah 6.

Opposition, it's telling us, is often stirred up when God's people are doing his work and building his kingdom. It may take various forms. The enemies began with an apparently innocent offer of help (v. 2). There was quite a bit of history behind the offer, however (see 2 Kings 17:24–41), and the leaders were discerning enough to know that this would lead to compromise and a loss of their identity as God's elect people, so the seemingly harsh rejection in verse 3 was justified. When that failed, the enemies discouraged the builders by using intimidation and bribery and by frustrating their efforts. Subsequently, they resorted to accusation and innuendo and sought to get the law to put a stop to the rebuilding (vv. 6–16; 5:3–10). In Nehemiah's day, the tactics of ridicule and armed force were added to their repertoire of opposition (Nehemiah 4:1–12). In the end, the opposition failed because 'the gracious hand of our God' was on them (Ezra 8:18) but it was not without its cost en route.

Western Christians have become used to enjoying freedom and privilege in their societies, but most Christians around the contemporary world regularly experience conflict and opposition, and have done for centuries. Given the teaching of the New Testament, we shouldn't expect it to be otherwise (Matthew 11:12; Acts 14:22; Ephesians 6:10–20).

4 Completion

Ezra 6:13–22

The opposition to the temple rebuilding backfired to Israel's advantage. The state archives, housed in Ecbatana, Cyrus' summer residence, and written in the official language of Aramaic, confirmed Israel's right to rebuild the temple (6:1–12). Moreover, Darius' response made it clear that the complainants' own treasury was to pay for the project, within the agreed limit (6:3–4), and that the command was enforceable on pain of dire punishment. So the work recommenced after nearly 20 years and took four and a half years to complete (v. 15).

Several features stand out regarding the completion of the work. The first is 'diligence', which was characteristic of the Jews, as might be expected, but was also required by Darius of his officials (5:8; 6:12–13). This was no leisure-time activity, to be done whenever people had nothing better to do.

Second, there is the 'preaching' of Haggai and Zechariah (v. 14). They played a vital role in establishing priorities and motivating dispirited settlers to build something worthy of God, even if it was more modest than their previous temple. Fortunately we have a record of their preaching in the books that bear their names. Third, the same stress is laid on working 'according to the command of the God of Israel' (vv. 14, 18) as we have seen previously. Even though Darius' words and God's words coincided at this point, the builders saw their work primarily as obeying God.

Fourth, the inauguration was a 'dedication' of the temple and the priests and Levites (vv. 16–18). The same diligence shown in the building project was now to be shown in offering worship. The main celebration feast, soon after completion, was the Passover (vv. 19–22), appropriately recalling the earlier seminal act of liberation. Yet none of this was done out of mere 'duty', and so we find a fifth repeated word: it was a celebration of 'joy' (vv. 16, 22).

Given the stress on 'separation' under Ezra's later leadership, one other note is of great significance here. The celebrations were not confined to the Jews but were open to anyone, provided they 'had separated themselves from the unclean practices of their Gentile neighbours' (v. 21). The builders were inclusive and welcoming but simultaneously uncompromising about what they believed and practised. In this they are a model for the contemporary church.

5 'This Ezra'

Ezra 7:1–10

At long last, 60 years after the last events, Ezra makes his appearance, and the story becomes more of a personal testimony than a historical record. While much of this chapter is taken up with Artaxerxes' letter, the focus throughout is on 'this Ezra' (v. 6) and his special qualities.

No one could function as a priest unless they had the right pedigree, and Ezra certainly had that (vv. 1–5). He could trace his family tree back to Aaron, through remarkable characters like Zadok and Phinehas. Priestly leadership was in his blood. Yet the work of a priest had necessarily undergone change since Aaron's day, not least because the priests were no longer able to preside over sacrifices in exile. As a result, teaching the law had become even more significant than before. Ezra took that responsibility seriously and was 'well versed' or 'skilled' (NRSV) in the law (v. 6). The word literally means 'rapid', which suggests that he was quick to grasp and understand the law's teaching. Verse 10 especially presents him as an ideal teacher and model for the scribes, whose later role was built, if not always well, on Ezra's work. Before he taught others, he studied the law himself and obeyed it personally. Would that all teachers followed his example!

Ezra is sometimes considered an overly sensitive, pious, even precious character, but this chapter portrays him differently. Since 'the king had granted him everything he asked' (v. 6) and provided such generous support and public affirmation for his leadership (vv. 21–26), he must have been a winsome person. In addition, he didn't suffer from the scholar's besetting sin of being an armchair critic who safely avoids action. He left his comfortable situation in Babylon and undertook a dangerous journey of just under a thousand miles at the hottest time of the year, to lead a disparate group back to their rugged homeland. He makes nothing of the arduous nature of the journey but passes over the four-month journey as if it was a day-trip to the seaside (v. 9).

Before we idolise Ezra, however, we must note that he recognises that his journey was protected and his mission successful because 'the hand of the Lord his God was on him' (vv. 6, 28). Success wasn't due to his charismatic leadership but to his great God.

6 Intermarriage

Ezra 10:1–17

The temple having been rebuilt, Ezra's task was to rebuild the nation into a Torah (law)-observing people. Sometime after his return, he was confronted with an issue that brought that challenge to the surface: many men had married 'foreign women', contrary to the law.

When Ezra was told, his initial reaction was to take the burden on himself. He tore his own tunic, pulled his own hair out, wept, fasted and, although appalled, shared in the guilt of others (9:3–7; 10:1). Only when the people themselves confessed their sin did Ezra take action, although he apparently had to be stirred into action by others (vv. 1–4). After an initial rain-soaked, centralised attempt at dealing with the issue, they decided to set up a national system by which the people who had married women from neighbouring nations illegitimately could swiftly set matters right (vv. 9–17). Intermarriage was a grievous sin because it threatened to undermine the very existence and identity of Israel by compromising its religious purity. If they wanted to repeat King Solomon's errors (1 Kings 11:1–13), why had God 'for a brief moment' shown his kindness in bringing them to their homeland (9:8–9)? What was the point?

Ralph Klein claims, 'It is difficult to find redeeming theological value in the chapter' ('Ezra', p. 746). It certainly is a challenging chapter. To us, living in a tolerant age that demonises any form of discrimination, Ezra's insistence that those who had married foreign women should divorce them seems inexplicably harsh and nonsensical. But we need first to ask how the original participants would have understood such verses, rather than asking how we should judge them from our 21st-century perspective.

Of course, we worry about the divorced women. Who was to care for them? How were they to survive? The answer, almost certainly, was that they would return to their extended families in the neighbouring nations and be looked after there.

The theological value of this chapter lies in the fact that it teaches us the vital importance of holiness among God's people. It may seem stark, harsh and disturbing to us, but maybe that's because we don't consider it very important to be holy (which originally meant being separated to serve God alone). Yet God still commands his people, 'Be holy, because I am holy' (Leviticus 19:2; 1 Peter 1:16).

Guidelines

Ezra may be read as a pattern for the people of God who are undergoing renewal after a period of exile, much like the church in our own day. Its primary stress is on the activity of God, without which no return or rebuilding would have happened. But God moved Cyrus' heart and placed his 'good hand' on his people and their leaders. Any growth or renewal that doesn't start here is of no value.

Yet, the people had their part to play. While not everyone joined in (see 8:15), many did, and we learn of the united and diligent way they undertook the task. We also learn that they stuck it out patiently, maintaining the vision and not being defeated by the waves of discouraging opposition they met. Reading Ezra in association with Haggai and Zechariah, we can also learn how much the people had to adapt to a new and more modest day instead of perpetually looking back to the 'glory days' of Solomon's temple.

Ezra also has much to teach us about the challenge of inclusion and exclusivity. While the people rightly included others in their celebration of the Passover (6:21), they had to be wary of unthinking inclusivism that might undermine their spiritual identity and their calling as the holy people of God. The book of Ezra gives no encouragement to racial or cultural discrimination today but it does challenge the contemporary church to consider how we might be a welcoming church without detriment to our own calling as a holy and distinct people, obedient to Jesus.

FURTHER READING

Ralph W. Klein, 'Ezra', *New Interpreters' Bible*, Vol. 3, Abingdon Press, 1999.

J.G. McConville, *Ezra, Nehemiah and Esther* (Daily Study Bible), Westminster John Knox, 1985.

H.G.M. Williamson, *Ezra, Nehemiah* (Word Biblical Commentary), Word, 1985.

Nehemiah

The book of Nehemiah is part two of 'Ezra–Nehemiah', which is seen as a single book in ancient tradition and by most contemporary scholars. This title reflects the two major characters, Ezra the scholar and Nehemiah the governor. They are both fascinating personalities, examples of how God can use people who are strikingly different in both role and temperament. The narrative portrays both as men of God; Ezra's characteristic phrase is 'our God' (Ezra 8:17–22; 9:8–13), while Nehemiah often speaks of 'my God' (Nehemiah 2:8, 12, 18; 13:14, 22, 29). But their approaches to leadership differ: when facing a crisis over the intermarriage of Jews with the surrounding peoples, Ezra resorts to confession of his people's sins, pulling out his own hair; Nehemiah, facing a similar crisis, chooses direct action, pulling out other people's hair (Ezra 9:3; Nehemiah 13:23–25)! However, the focus of the book is less on these leaders than on the community of God's people as a whole, as they seek to rebuild their life together after the exile, both physically and spiritually.

Some books are easier to read than others. This one offers a curious mixture: a lively, fast-paced narrative that grips our attention is disrupted by lists of names, which can seem dry and dull. Most of the time, Nehemiah himself is the narrator, so it reads like a personal memoir, but chapters 8:1—12:26 tell us about Nehemiah and others from someone else's perspective. All this indicates that different sources have been brought together to form the book by its final author/editor: tradition says that this was Ezra himself, but we cannot be sure.

There are also links with Chronicles, particularly in the opening words (Ezra 1:1–4 is identical to the closing words of 2 Chronicles), and their shared interest in the temple, liturgical prayers and music. Were all these books written by the same person? On balance, probably not, due to their differences. Chronicles' interest in the prophets and the Davidic dynasty is not a feature of Ezra–Nehemiah; also, Chronicles does not mention Solomon's sins involving many wives, while Nehemiah 13:26 uses Solomon as an example of the dangers of mixed marriage.

Quotations are taken from the New Revised Standard Version of the Bible.

1 Pleading boldly with the King of kings

Nehemiah 1:1–11

About 100 years have passed since Cyrus the Persian conquered the Babylonian empire and encouraged exiles from Judah to return to their homeland. Different groups have returned over the years, and some have built a new, smaller temple on the site of the old one in Jerusalem (Ezra 3:7–13).

Thirteen years after Ezra himself joined the returnees in Jerusalem (Ezra 7:1–10), news of further developments there reaches Susa, one of the major cities of the Persian empire. Nehemiah's family are among those who have not returned, and he has been building a successful career in the Persian civil service. But this news shocks him: those in Jerusalem who are 'left from the exile' (which could include both returnees from Babylon and some who were never exiled, survivors in Judah) are in a bad way. Jerusalem's defences have been destroyed; this is news, so presumably it has happened in some military action quite recently, perhaps of the kind depicted in Ezra 4:17–23. Here is potentially a matter of life and death for a small, vulnerable community in an unstable corner of the empire.

Nehemiah could choose to wring his hands, shrug the news off and get on with his comfortable life, but he makes a different choice, and it begins with prayer. Like the exiled psalmist who refused to forget Jerusalem (Psalm 137:5–6), Nehemiah mourns as if someone he loves has died.

Nehemiah (the name means 'Yahweh has comforted') appeals to Yahweh as the God of covenant commitment (v. 5), through promises made in the time of Moses. But covenant is a two-way commitment, and Nehemiah is painfully aware that his people have been wayward and unreliable in their attitude to Yahweh. It might be tempting to excuse himself, but instead he confesses, identifying with his people's failings.

He repeatedly presents himself and his people as God's servants—an ironic term, in light of their repeated rebellions against their divine master. Yet Nehemiah counts himself among some true 'servants' who delight to revere Yahweh's name. The test of these noble words will be in how he acts, and he has a plan—but it will require boldness on his part and a compassionate response from his master, the Persian king.

2 Pleading boldly with an earthly king

Nehemiah 2:1–10

As the king's butler, Nehemiah is an important member of the royal staff: he brings wine to the king and tastes it to check it has not been poisoned. Perhaps the king has come to trust him as a confidant and adviser. This privileged access gives him an opportunity to present his plan to the one whose permission is needed for it to succeed, but kings can be dangerously unpredictable, as other Old Testament books, such as Daniel and Esther, show. Court etiquette seems to have required a cheerful disposition, with personal problems laid aside; revealing his unhappiness to his earthly master could be highly risky, but Nehemiah does so, perhaps quite deliberately.

The king quizzes Nehemiah about his very evident sadness. Here is his opportunity; he grasps it, though initially with caution. He makes no mention of politically sensitive issues, such as rebuilding the walls of a conquered city with a history of rebellion. He presents a more general and personal concern, more likely to resonate with the king: the burial place of one's ancestors (2:5) was regarded as a place deserving of respect in that culture.

The king takes the bait, asking what Nehemiah wants. But how can a mere servant, whose role is to do the king's bidding, possibly expect his master to do *his* bidding? For Nehemiah's outrageously bold plan to succeed, a minor miracle is needed. He turns to Yahweh, firing off a brief 'arrow prayer' before explaining his request. His activism is grounded in prayer, as we saw in the less hurried example of the opening chapter. Later we find him repeatedly asking God to 'remember me' (5:19; 13:14, 22, 31) or 'remember them' (6:14; 13:29), in words similar to some in the Psalms, and also joining in corporate prayers of penitence (ch. 9) as well as joyful communal celebration (12:27–43).

In a bold act of faith, Nehemiah requests both royal authorisation and expensive resources for the project, and now refers to restoring the city's fortifications (vv. 7–8). The queen is mentioned as sitting alongside the king; does her presence influence the king's decision? We cannot tell—but ultimately it is 'the gracious hand of my God upon me' that Nehemiah sees as decisive. He is granted what he requests, along with an armed escort—a providential bonus, as we begin to hear the first rumours of opposition to his project.

3 Builders together

Nehemiah 2:11—3:32

Nehemiah soon sets to work after the long journey from Susa (north of the Persian Gulf) to Jerusalem. Assessing the scale of the project is his first challenge, which is best done secretly and alone; he wants maximum surprise impact, to wrong-foot his opponents and excite potential allies.

Next comes a greater challenge—envisioning and motivating local people, who may have become blind or apathetic towards their situation and needs. Nehemiah appeals to them on different levels, seeking to arouse their sense of shame that God's holy city should be in such a state, as well as testifying to his awareness of God's hand on the work, not to mention having royal backing. His arguments, along with his personal conviction and enthusiasm, prove infectious, prompting a positive response—and the expected opposition.

A fifth-century BC document from a Jewish community in Egypt mentions Sanballat as governor of Samaria; his rule may have extended to Jerusalem. Tobiah the Ammonite seems to be one of Sanballat's subordinates—perhaps his deputy in Jerusalem. Little wonder that they feel threatened by this newly arrived interloper and want to accuse him of political rebellion (2:19). Nehemiah responds to their scorn and accusations with resolute determination; he points to divine rather than royal support as the source of his confidence (v. 20).

The list of Nehemiah's co-workers in chapter 3 may initially seem tedious, but the details give glimpses of a fascinating mixture of people. Here are priests, nobles and officials, alongside merchants, artisans and other ordinary people, both men and women (v. 12). No doubt, self-interest plays a part, as people build fortifications near their own homes; yet some of the workers come from places beyond Jerusalem, such as Jericho and Tekoa, Gibeon and Mizpah. All bring skills and life experience, yet none brings any expertise that seems suited to the enterprise: no engineers or builders are mentioned alongside the goldsmiths and perfumers. Some have the energy and resources to repair more than one section (vv. 19, 20, 24). A few decline to pull their weight (v. 5), in contrast to the many others who are willing to roll up their sleeves and do the mundane, physically demanding work. In this roll of honour, no one is singled out and praised above the others; it truly is a team effort and is celebrated as such by the writer's meticulous account.

4 Facing mockery and threats

Nehemiah 4

The scale of opposition grows: first we met Sanballat and Tobiah (2:10), then they were joined by Geshem the Arab (2:19); now we hear mention of the Samarian army, more Arabs, Ammonites and Ashdodites (4:2, 7). The workers in Jerusalem seem increasingly encircled by hostile and powerful forces—enough to raise anxieties and sap the will. Their opponents resort to scorn; being laughed at on account of your hard work can be very demoralising. Sanballat's observation is quite correct; building anything out of burnt rubble is a huge challenge. His question 'Will they finish today? (v. 2) might niggle at the weary builders as they wonder if they will ever get the job done.

In that situation, one response might be to try to give the tormentors a bloody nose; perhaps Nehemiah and others dream wistfully of sending a hit squad to Samaria. Instead, his response is to pray (vv. 4–5). What might sound to us like a vengeful prayer is more about handing over to God the desire for revenge and trusting God to deal with the matter, so that God's honour will be upheld. Nehemiah reminds himself (and his fellow builders) where their true hope lies. Intimidation has failed; they press on with the job and close the circle of the wall. Morale is boosted when they realise that the halfway point in the project has been reached (v. 6).

The struggle intensifies, however; now an armed attack seems imminent, and morale slumps again. Those among the builders who come from beyond Jerusalem perhaps receive calls to return home (verse 12 can be translated in this way) to protect their families in this time of growing instability. Nehemiah responds first (as usual) with prayer, and then with practical action: 'we prayed to our God and set a guard' (v. 9). Next he addresses the key issue of morale, speaking encouragement and challenge, reminding people of the greatness of their God, who 'will fight for us' (v. 20). The workers labour on, handicapped by the need to wield weapons as well as tools. As ever, Nehemiah is not safe in comfort behind the lines, but in the thick of the action at the danger points, alongside those he leads.

5 Protecting the vulnerable

Nehemiah 5

Nehemiah finds leadership full of challenges, sometimes coming from unexpected directions. Suddenly the narrative shifts its focus from external threats to an internal one—a crisis within the community.

Ordinary people are struggling to survive. One of the various causes is probably Nehemiah's wall-building project, which is a drain on resources. Time spent on the rebuilding inevitably means less time and energy for working in the family business or on the farm, with profits and harvests reduced as a result. Another factor is taxation to fund the Persian empire (including salaries for local governors, such as Nehemiah). Perhaps most disturbing of all, some of the wealthier local people are taking advantage of fellow Jews who are economically vulnerable, using the opportunity to charge them interest on loans, exploit their families as labourers and take their land in payment for debts.

Nehemiah is shocked and outraged. Anger motivates him to action—tempered by the wisdom to 'think it over' a little first (v. 7). He confronts the influential people, the heads of families and overseers of the work, who seem blind or indifferent to their failings. Perhaps Nehemiah himself is convicted: verse 10 may indicate that his own lending practices need rethinking. The Torah encouraged the more fortunate to help those who fell on hard times, which could include providing loans and accepting work from their family members as payment. But this was done as part of the family of God's people: exploiting and making money out of your own wider family's struggles was unthinkable. Nehemiah opts for open discussion and public confrontation. Having established a consensus that the current situation is unjust and unacceptable, he presses his point to achieve an immediate response.

Practising what you preach is always crucial, to avoid accusations of hypocrisy. Nehemiah chooses transparency, putting the record straight about his own lifestyle. Provincial governors such as him were entitled to live in some style and comfort, and they usually did. Nehemiah chooses to sacrifice some of his rights and opportunities, lest they become a burden on vulnerable people. These choices involve some personal cost, making demands on his own resources. Underlying his brusque leadership style is a mixture of reverence for God and compassion for his people (vv. 15, 18).

6 Whom can you trust?

Nehemiah 6

With the building project approaching completion, the opposition changes tack. Intimidation through mockery and threats of violence have failed, so now they try rumour, deception and intrigue.

The invitation from Sanballat and Geshem has a plausible, accommodating tone: they suggest meeting Nehemiah halfway between Samaria and Jerusalem, at Ono (v. 2). The way to negotiation seems to be opening up, but the journey would take Nehemiah away from the building work for several days. In addition, the open countryside could be a dangerous place for travellers: he might mysteriously come to a violent end at the hands of bandits. He opts for caution and finds the pressure increasing relentlessly (v. 4). Now the rumours begin (fuelled by a letter deliberately left unsealed), with a personal smear campaign against him. Again, it has a plausible ring: with their defences restored, the people of Jerusalem might look to their proud history of independence and seek to re-establish their cherished monarchy. Who would be better placed to lead such a rebellion than Nehemiah, the governor who instigated the rebuilding?

Nehemiah holds his nerve, turning to God for strength once again (v. 9), but perhaps the pressure is beginning to get to him. Can a man of God help to steady and strengthen his resolve? He consults Shemaiah, who has a godly manner (his words in verse 10 have the cadence of poetry, the rhythm often used for oracles from God in the Old Testament), but

Shemaiah's words need to be weighed. For a layman such as Nehemiah to go into the central areas of the temple was forbidden in the Torah, so this action might well lead to his being discredited and even killed. Nehemiah refuses to panic and sees through the pious God-talk: here is a paid agent of his enemies, one of a number among the religious establishment of Jerusalem (vv. 13–14).

The web of intrigue and intimidation among the city's elite includes other leaders who owe loyalty to Tobiah; they add to the morale-sapping propaganda campaign (vv. 17–19). Yet in spite of it all, the rebuilding of the wall is completed. Nehemiah and many others see God's hand in their achievement, but the narrative is clear that God chooses to work through Nehemiah and his co-labourers. It is human perseverance and hard work, inspired and energised by God, that has produced this outcome.

Guidelines

Faithful discipleship invariably brings struggles and battles that require perseverance. The first half of the book of Nehemiah highlights challenges particularly relevant to those in positions of influence and responsibility. There may be a buzz of excitement and anxiety as a new challenge unfolds. How do you cope effectively under relentless pressure to make decisions and get the job done? In the rush to reach the targets, do you remember to celebrate what has already been achieved?

For leaders, Nehemiah himself provides a striking example of a transformational individual. He is a thoughtful, careful planner who exercises shrewd judgement, yet can also seize the moment suddenly and boldly. He is a practical visionary, who knows how to inspire and motivate others, and can also organise them to work effectively together, adjusting the plan when the situation changes and new needs emerge. He learns how to recognise and respond to threats, sometimes from unexpected quarters, and to cope with misunderstanding and smear campaigns while still sustaining people's morale. He leads by example, offering integrity and hard work, trustworthiness and reliability. Prayer and action go hand in hand, in a natural and continuous synergy. He also has an abrasiveness and a confrontational style that would not prove fruitful in all situations. The consultative style of the apostles and elders seen in Acts 15, involving an element of compromise, provides a very different model of leadership.

Although we see things from Nehemiah's perspective, the story is not really about him. It's about how God rebuilds his people after a massive trauma and in times that remain very challenging. Building community involves working together towards a God-given vision and resisting opportunities to exploit those who are vulnerable.

1 Learning God's teaching

Nehemiah 8

Ezra the scholar now appears on the scene. He speaks from a specially constructed platform, indicating an event that has been planned by the community's leaders (v. 4); yet he waits to be called for by the people (v. 1)—their hunger for God's word is also important. Ezra reads from a 'Torah' ('law' or 'teaching') scroll. Gathering, writing and editing their treasured memories and traditions was a major concern for some of the Jews during their exile in Babylon, and this scroll is probably one of the fruits of that labour. The responses of the people in this and the following chapter suggest that they are listening to teaching from Deuteronomy and Leviticus. The reading takes place not with a select few in the temple but in a public square. It is to be heard by all who can understand—men, women and children.

The need not simply to hear but also to understand is repeatedly emphasised. Part of the process involves small-group work, as Levites move among the crowd, explaining and 'giving the sense' of what has been heard—perhaps a mixture of teaching and responding to people's questions. (Some traditions suggest that the Levites were translating the Hebrew scroll into Aramaic.)

This teaching of Yahweh provokes powerful responses. People weep, possibly at the contrast between what they have heard and the lives they have been living. There are times to mourn at our failings, but also times to rejoice in God's grace: Ezra insists that this is a day for communal celebration. In the book of Exodus, God gives commands and a call to holiness, but only after graciously calling his people and saving them from slavery in Egypt. Sometimes people need to be reminded how they have been saved and encouraged to rejoice at God's goodness.

One of the reminders turns out to be a very physical learning experience. This seventh month is harvest time, when farmers build temporary tents or bivouacs so that they can maximise time spent in the fields and protect their crops from storms or theft. Those bivouacs can be reminders of the way their ancestors lived after the exodus from Egypt, travelling in the desert. So now the city dwellers do something similar, building temporary shelters as a way to remember and celebrate all that God has given them, in the exodus from Egypt (and more recently from Babylon), as well as in the current harvest from their fields in the promised land.

2 Confessing our sins

Nehemiah 9

There are times to dance—and times to mourn. The narrative moves abruptly from the festival celebration of the previous chapter to mourning and confession of sin: both extremes are appropriate in the life of God's people as they hear and respond to God's words. Both responses need to be heartfelt and can be expressed in outward, physical ways. Those who mourn deeply may not feel hungry or to bother about their physical appearance (v. 1); the people prostrate themselves in abject confession, but are then raised from grovelling or self-pity to stand upright before God (vv. 2–5).

The celebration in chapter 8 focused primarily on God's gracious actions for the people. The lengthy prayer in chapter 9 (ascribed to Ezra in some translations but not in the Hebrew text, which suggests, rather, that it is prayed by the Levites) does something similar. Appealing directly to God as 'you', it begins with praise for Yahweh's eternal greatness and life-giving, creative power. Shaped by what has been heard in Ezra's reading of the Torah, the prayer goes on to revisit the story of Yahweh's dealings with Abram and his descendants. Their waywardness and repeated rebellion inevitably come into focus again and again; yet still it is the good news of Yahweh's forgiving and rescuing grace that is emphasised. Glorifying God, rather than shaming God's people, is the prayer's strongest undercurrent. God is to be praised in all things, including his acts of judgement—not an easy thing to do when that judgement has so deep an impact on us.

How can a book that centres on the heroism of a Persian governor give such a negative picture of life under Persian rule, involving slavery and exploitation (vv. 36–37)? This prayer acknowledges God's justice in allowing his people to suffer for their sins (vv. 33, 37), yet it refuses to concede that living as serfs, enriching foreign overlords with the fruit of the promised land, can ever be an adequate fulfilment of God's promise and purpose. Yahweh is still 'our God', the saving God of the exodus, Mount Sinai and covenant love (vv. 12, 17, 32; see Exodus 34:6–7); this God will still hear a direct appeal by those who are honest about their own failings.

3 Commitment to change

Nehemiah 9:38—10:39

The prayer in chapter 9 was one of repentance. A sign of true repentance is the willingness and desire to change, so those who are praying now commit themselves to radical transformation in their behaviour.

The Torah that Ezra has been reading speaks into a wide range of life situations, reflected in the specific concerns that are now mentioned. Yahweh's people must be 'separated to God's teaching', the Torah (10:28). The concern about intermarriage is not a case of ethnic and racial prejudice, as it might sound to us; religious distinctiveness is the key issue. Developing such deep and lasting ties with those who worshipped other gods inevitably led to some degree of involvement in their religions, eroding the exclusive loyalty to which Yahweh had called his people; the experience of King Solomon was a notorious example (see 13:25–27). There could also be socio-economic consequences of intermarriage, such as the loss of family land.

Keeping the sabbath is another of the distinctive commitments of Yahweh's people that might be undermined by interaction with other peoples (particularly commerce with them), so this aspect of their identity is also reinforced (v. 31). Supporting the ongoing worship of Yahweh in the temple is a further key priority (otherwise, what was the point of rebuilding?), so the community commits itself to regular giving, both in cash and in kind. There are numerous aspects of worship in the temple that need regular resourcing, in addition to the upkeep of the building: support for personnel, along with offerings and fuel, are highlighted here. Bearing in mind some of the economic pressures and struggles that we glimpsed earlier (5:1–5), the personal sacrifices involved in these promises are not to be underestimated. Commitments are invariably costly, not just as a one-off but on an ongoing basis.

Who makes this commitment? This list of names at the start of chapter 10 is extensive and wide-ranging, including both individuals and whole families. It reflects a culture in which leadership was largely the domain of men, yet it insists that God speaks to all. Men, women and children are able to hear God's teaching and respond to it together as a community, with transformed lives resulting (v. 28; see 8:2). Together they make a solemn promise to 'walk' (that is, 'live') by God's teaching (v. 29).

4 Honouring the pioneers

Nehemiah 11

Jerusalem is 'the holy city'—an evocative phrase, found twice in this chapter (vv. 1, 18). This is a place where God has chosen to be present and known in a particular way (see 1:9). Its walls have been repaired and the nature of God's holiness has been proclaimed in the words read by Ezra from the Torah scroll. Yet ultimately a city is not just about its stones, gates or scrolls, but about its people. God's holy city needs people who live up to that name, holy people who will reflect Yahweh's character.

So we come to another of this book's lists of names. Like the lists of wall builders (ch. 3), returnees (ch. 7), those who responded to the Torah (ch. 10) and worship leaders (ch. 12), this long record of names is one that we might find puzzling and dull, and we may choose to pass over it with barely a glance. But some of the first people to read or hear this book would have recognised with pride, in these various rolls of honour, the names of their parents or grandparents. Valuing those whose commitment and hard work have produced things of lasting worth, things that have been inherited and enjoyed by subsequent generations, is an important discipline for any community. It honours good people for their faith, hope and love, and can help to foster gratitude along with a sense of perspective. Without it, complacency may set in and things get taken for granted. People need some sense of attachment to previous generations, to help them make sense of the present and decide their priorities for the future.

Zechariah had prophesied that Jerusalem would flourish to the extent of overflowing with people and animals (Zechariah 2:1–5); the leaders of Judah now set about making that vision a reality. The exact process is unclear: were some chosen by lot (v. 1) while others volunteered (v. 2)? Or are these two verses talking about the same people, being commended because of their willingness to respond when the lot fell on them? Either way, their dedication to this pioneering role, and the sacrifices it may have involved, are highlighted in this chapter.

5 Celebrating and dedicating

Nehemiah 12:27–47

Significant achievements are worth noticing and celebrating. The completion of the wall is an impressive triumph, which merits a big celebration. Spontaneous, unplanned responses can be ideal in some situations, but this event involves a lot of planning and organising, in order to ensure that many people are involved and that its symbolic impact is maximised.

The scene is painted vividly for us. Two processions climb up on to the walls on the west side of the city and head off in opposite directions, one towards the north and the other to the south. A noisy team of singers and musicians, gathered from far and wide, leads each procession, perhaps echoing each other antiphonally (singing alternate lines or verses of the worship songs). Behind them walk leaders of the community, including priests (who add to the fanfare, vv. 35–36). There is nothing half-hearted about the celebration as they all delight in what their people have achieved with God's enabling (v. 43). The two groups 'beat the bounds' of the city, following the walls round towards the east, where they meet again, this time at the temple.

This final meeting place has been carefully chosen, for the celebration is also a dedication (v. 27), a term more commonly used not of walls but of altars or temples. The rebuilt temple was dedicated for God's presence and use (Ezra 6), and the references to purification and sacrifices here in Nehemiah (vv. 30, 43) remind us of that earlier ceremony. The walls designate the bounds of Jerusalem, the holy city; dedicating the walls helps to express that sense of holiness for the place and its people. With this ceremony, the new life of the holy city truly begins.

In these verses we have rejoined the first-person 'Nehemiah memoir', which we last saw in chapter 7. The chronological order of events may not always follow the narrative order of the book; for example, did the move to populate the city, described in chapter 11, actually happen after the dedication of the walls, as some have argued? This seems possible, and we cannot say for sure. Some scholars question further whether Nehemiah and Ezra were really contemporaries, but the plain reading of this passage indicates that they were (vv. 26, 36–38; see also 8:9).

6 Frustrations and battles

Nehemiah 13

If only yesterday's passage could have ended the book! After the worshipful euphoria of the wall-dedication, this final chapter seems like an anticlimax. It shows Nehemiah back in his administrative role as governor, battling on to sort out a succession of frustrating, mundane problems.

Some of these issues have arisen during Nehemiah's absence. After a spell back in Persia (perhaps to give a report on his twelve years in Jerusalem), Nehemiah returns for a further period as governor. He finds that his old opponents, Tobiah and Sanballat, have taken advantage of his absence to assert their influence and authority again through some of their old alliances in Jerusalem's influential circles. Nehemiah's fighting spirit has not been cooled by his years of experience, and he takes decisive action (vv. 7–9, 28).

Is Nehemiah unduly concerned that people should keep the rules? In one sense, that is his job as governor, but his deeper concern is for the welfare of his people. He remembers the disobedience of previous generations, which led to Yahweh's judgement on them in the trauma of the exile, and warns his generation not to forget it (vv. 18, 26). God's people are called to a holy lifestyle, expressed in distinctives such as keeping the sabbath. Turning it into just another working and trading day is a betrayal of their commitment to live God's way. Neglecting their commitment to pay their worship leaders, so that the latter return to their family farms to avoid starvation, is equally unacceptable (vv. 10–12). Marriage to foreigners who do not worship Yahweh, where it leads to involvement in their religions, is another betrayal that must be avoided (vv. 1–3, 23–27). The promises that people made earlier (ch. 10) need to be honoured.

Ezra's approach to mixed marriages was radical, requiring divorce (Ezra 10). If Nehemiah faces the same problem later, why does he not require the same response? Perhaps the social consequences of Ezra's policy were so severe that a less stringent response is now deemed preferable. All these decisions require difficult judgements, which repeatedly drive Nehemiah to prayer (vv. 14, 22, 29, 31). There may be hints of anxiety and uncertainty in these prayers; even the most godly leader cannot be sure of always being right. Nehemiah strives prayerfully in his commitment to God and trusts that God's commitment to him surpasses everything else (v. 22).

Guidelines

Like the first half of the book, its closing chapter gives glimpses of the demands and challenges of leadership, particularly as old problems, which seemed to be in the past, rear their heads afresh. The challenge to persevere prayerfully continues, facing up to hard decisions in the light of what we know of God's character and word.

For all his charisma and vision, Nehemiah cannot lead alone. We have seen others emerge, with different gifts and roles: Hanani and Hananiah (7:2), Ezra, various Levites and priests, heads of clans, and leaders of the Jerusalem community and the wider province. These groups and individuals need to learn how to interact, building mutual trust and shared objectives as they work out the complex realities of their situation. Effective leadership needs this corporate dimension.

God speaking to God's people is another theme prominent in the second part of the book. Ezra's role in this is crucial as he brings forward and opens what is now part of our scriptures. The preacher/teacher's calling is to enable people of all ages to hear and understand God's word and respond to it. That response needs to come from the heart, involving more than simply fine prayers. Repentance means a willingness to change behaviour in all areas of life, involving work and commercial activity, close relationships and our commitment to the worshipping community. Disciples are called to a distinctive life as a holy people.

Joyful celebration is another part of our calling. It can come with marking the seasons, such as harvest, and with hearing God's word and its central message of God's saving grace. Faithful workers, not least pioneers, are people to be named, recognised and honoured. Particular significant achievements, done with God's enabling help, are further causes for celebration, not to be missed.

FURTHER READING

T. Bolin, *Ezra, Nehemiah*, Liturgical Press, 2012.

J. Goldingay, *Ezra, Nehemiah and Esther for Everyone*, SPCK, 2013.

D. Kidner, *Ezra and Nehemiah*, IVP, 2009.

H. Williamson, *Ezra, Nehemiah*, Word, 2010.

Galatians

The letter of Paul to the Galatians is less than 150 verses but its enormous influence on Christianity has been out of all proportion to its size. Coming to us from the earliest days of Christianity, Galatians is the most passionate of Paul's letters, driven by the issue of how Galatian Gentile Christians should relate to the Jewish law, especially circumcision.

Paul's authorship of Galatians has never been seriously questioned, but there is debate about whether the recipients were ethnic Galatians (from north Galatia) or people belonging to the Roman province of Galatia (south Galatia), both in modern Turkey. Conclusions on this point affect the dating of the letter as well (either as late as AD56 or as early as 48/49), since it depends on how Paul's movements in Galatians and Acts are reconciled.

Most good theology is polemic—that is, it responds to the questions and debates of its time. Galatians is especially polemical in that Paul is responding to those he terms 'agitators' (5:12, NIV) who are trying to compel Paul's Galatian converts to be circumcised (6:12). Although Paul is somewhat cryptic about their identity, from clues in Galatians we can infer that they were Jewish Christian missionaries with a theology that required circumcision for men if they were to be proper Christians. Paul does not hold back in describing this position as a perversion of the gospel of Christ (1:7). It is worth bearing in mind that within the Greco-Roman culture of the time, circumcision and other Jewish practices were looked down on as rather primitive, so circumcision for Gentiles was not a culturally easy option. So for Paul to say that circumcision meant nothing (5:6; 6:15) might be construed as an attempt to preach a cheap, watered-down sort of gospel—'people-pleasing' in Paul's own words (1:10). So Paul makes his rooted, contextual theological case, fizzing with the profound themes of the cross, faith, law, grace, promise, freedom and love.

Quotations are taken from the New Revised Standard Version of the Bible, unless otherwise stated.

1 The gospel and the apostle

Galatians 1

Paul is bursting to get on with his themes of gospel and especially apostleship in this chapter—so much so that he can't even complete his initial greeting without interrupting himself (v. 1). Here his passionate polemic begins to address the questions of his critics. Through whose authority has Paul been sent? None other than that of Jesus Christ and God the Father.

Paul's theological starting point is given in verse 4 as the gospel in miniature. He draws on standard Jewish categories of the two ages—this present age and the age to come. In giving himself 'for our sins', Jesus Christ has rescued us from the power of this evil age and brought us under the power of his Lordship. Such a gospel is needed, since it leads into Paul's broadside against the Galatians in verse 6. In all other Pauline letters, this would be the thanksgiving slot, but for the churches of Galatia it is a sharp reprimand. Paul's sense of shock at their turncoat behaviour is clearly evident. Why is he 'astonished'? Because, by insisting that Gentile converts must follow Jewish practices such as circumcision, the false teachers have shifted the basis of salvation to 'the gospel plus… something else'. Such additions undermine the graced nature of the gospel (v. 6). The key point in verses 6–10, then, is that the gospel headlined in verse 4 has a divine authority that is not dependent on 'some who are confusing you' (v. 7), or on Paul and his team, or even on 'an angel from heaven' (v. 8). The preacher does not need to generate the power of the gospel.

In verses 11–24, Paul continues his case for the divine origin of his apostleship, stressing his initial independence from Jerusalem and its human authorities, as well as his exemplary credentials within Judaism (vv. 13–14). The 'revelation of Jesus Christ' to Paul (v. 12) on the Damascus road (see Acts 9) was both a conversion and a commissioning, also proffering personal encounter with Christ as a sufficient criterion for apostleship.

Paul's mention of the later 'visit' (v. 18, literally, 'getting to know someone') to Cephas (Peter) raises the issue of the tension with the Jerusalem church which becomes evident in chapter 2.

2 Crucified with Christ

Galatians 2

If 1:4 set the theological benchmark for chapter 1, then 2:19–20 provides the theological rationale for what comes before. 'I have been [and continue to be] crucified with Christ' means that our identity comes from Christ, not from 'the works of the law' (v. 16). This is why circumcision and catering arrangements occasion so much theology in Galatians. How will the growing number of Gentile Christians be included in what started as a Jewish Christian community? Mission is truly the mother of theology here, urging the articulation of 'the truth of the gospel' (vv. 5b, 14) for the church then and now.

This is a chapter of two halves, where autobiography merges with doctrine, although it is worth stressing that verses 15–21 are a direct continuation of the Antioch incident in verses 11–14: the more conciliatory 'we' of verse 15 refers to Paul and Peter. The news that Peter ate with Gentiles in Antioch is likely to have been reported in Jerusalem (v. 12a), where the church was under pressure from zealous Jews to observe the law. Despite Peter's good intentions in trying to avoid trouble for Jewish Christians in Jerusalem and Judea, his keeping separate from Gentiles at meal times sets off theological alarm bells for Paul. Peter's actions are building up what had been torn down (v. 18). Such 'play-acting' (or hypocrisy, v. 13) masked Peter's real convictions about how God justifies both Jews and Gentiles (vv. 15–16; see Acts 15:7–11). So we are introduced to the doctrinal mountains that are covered in the rest of the letter.

Verses 15–21 of this chapter were especially significant for the Protestant Reformers, thus also shaping subsequent Christian history and theology. Verse 16 states three times that we are not justified by the works of the law (echoing Psalm 143:2), and twice affirms that we are justified ('reckoned as righteous') through and by faith in Christ (and 'the faith *of* Christ'). What exactly is Paul opposing? The traditional understanding is that 'works of the law' are good deeds that gain merit with God. The danger here is that the Judaism of Paul's time can end up as a legalistic caricature. Newer perspectives understand 'the works of the law' to mean those aspects of the law that marked out Israel's identity. The marker of our new identity, then, is faith in the Son of God and entails mixed catering.

3 The blessing of Abraham

Galatians 3

Paul is indignant regarding the foolishness of the Galatians (vv. 1, 3). Having been set free by Christ from the 'present evil age' (1:4) and living now in the age to come by the power of the Spirit (vv. 2–3, 5), they have been 'bewitched'. The agitators may have spoken of 'ending' or bringing to perfection their faith through circumcision ('the flesh', v. 3). In an attempt to break the spell, Paul reminds the Galatians of how they entered into God's new age, contrasting Spirit and faith with flesh and law.

We reach the heart of Galatians from verse 6 onward. Paul quotes freely from the scriptures six times in verses 6–14 to show what God had intended all along (vv. 8, 11; see Habakkuk 2:4). Abraham believed God's covenant promise and so God 'reckoned it to him as righteousness' (Genesis 15:6). The promise was to bless through Abraham 'all the families of the earth' (Genesis 12:3). Therefore all the families of the earth who believe in that promise become part of the same family of faith. Paul is clear that if we rely on the law for our justification, it becomes a curse (Deuteronomy 27:26)—a curse that is exchanged with Christ so that we might know the blessing of Abraham (vv. 13–14).

Crucially, the promise made to Abraham came before the law, so the law cannot 'annul' the promise. What, then, is the purpose of the law? The law was 'ordained through angels' (v. 19), so it is something holy (Romans 7:12), designed to make us aware of sin, but it is an intermediary safety measure between the promise and its fulfilment. Through being imprisoned by the law, Israel is directed to the only escape route—the fulfilment of the promise in Christ. The law was a 'babysitter' (Wright, pp. 39–40) awaiting Abraham's offspring, Jesus Christ, who would be the mature representative of all who believe (the new 'children of God', v. 26). Consequently, ethnicity, gender, socio-economic status—or any other identity markers—are all irrelevant to our identity in Christ. Such radical equality sets the bar high for the family of faith, then and now.

4 'Abba! Father!'

For Jewish and Gentile Christians, Paul speaks of their journey out of slavery under the law (v. 2, the law being like 'guardians and trustees') and out of slavery to 'beings that by nature are not gods' (v. 8) respectively. In an extraordinary move, Paul equates the law and all other 'gods' through the term 'elemental spirits' (*stoicheia*) (vv. 3, 9), broadly understood then as the cosmic forces or spirits that had power and influence over human lives. The journeys for Jewish and Gentile Christians are therefore parallel; they are both legal 'minors' (v. 1) until attaining their legal majority in the 'fullness of time' (v. 4), both spiritual orphans until Christ redeems them for adoption into God's one family (v. 5).

The evidence of this freedom is the reception of the Spirit. Paul switches his pronouns from the third person to the second person singular to underline the point (v. 6). Doctrine turns into experience when we cry, 'Abba! Father!'—an intimate, familiar name that Jesus also used (Mark 14:36; compare Romans 8:15–17). Our adoption and inheritance are accomplished by the work of God the Father, Son and Spirit (v. 6): note the trinitarian point being spelt out in this, one of Christianity's earliest documents.

The second section of the chapter, verses 12–20, strikes a more pastoral tone, which was missing at the beginning of the letter. The extent of the previous goodwill between the Galatians and Paul becomes very clear, as well as Paul's anguish over the change of affairs (vv. 15–16). Paul even uses the figure of spiritual motherhood, suggesting that the Galatians have made him go through labour pains a second time (v. 19). He is perplexed indeed (v. 20)!

Finally, in the third section of the chapter (vv. 21–31), Paul allegorises the story of Hagar and Sarah from Genesis 21:9–12, using interpretative methods common at the time. His purpose in doing so is explained from verse 21 onward: if they want to be subject to the law, they must listen to it and understand that the law itself awaits fulfilment and, therefore, freedom.

5 Free to bear fruit

We are free! This freedom comes by faith, in hope, and for love. Love is the fulfilment of the law, and love is possible only if we live by the Spirit. In so doing, we will bear fruit. This is the gist of Galatians 5.

In verses 2–4 Paul presents the Galatians with the starkest choice in the whole letter—Christ or circumcision. The latter is not a relatively minor completion of the gospel, as the 'agitators' might have said; rather, it is a sign of intention to take on the whole law. By contrast, the only thing that counts for us is faith, made effective through love. Our freedom is to be used in order to give loving service to one another, as captured in one of the great commandments (v. 13; see Leviticus 19:18; Matthew 22:36–40). Love sums up and fulfils the law. It puts the law in its proper perspective.

Christian freedom is distinct from many contemporary notions of freedom. It is not licence to do as we like; rather, it means to transfer our allegiance from one power to another, as the exodus language behind much of Galatians would indicate. Paul's opposition between Spirit and flesh in verses 16–26 is not suggesting that we are dual-natured humans, that human desires are necessarily wrong, that the material world is set against the non-material world, or that Spirit and flesh are equally matched. Again, he is drawing on the idea of 'two ages'—the power of this present evil age ('flesh') and the power of the age to come ('Spirit'). We have been crucified with Christ and been set free to live under the power of the Spirit. However, the two ages overlap and there is currently war between the two powers.

Paul lists 15 works of the flesh (vv. 19–21), of which eight have to do with conflict, broadly suggestive of the problems facing the Galatian church. Nine 'fruit of the Spirit' are given and it is no accident that 'love' comes first. 'Fruit' is singular here, suggesting that we are to grow in all of these virtues. If we keep in step with the Spirit, the fruit will grow.

6 Fulfil the Law of Christ

'Let us not become conceited' (5:26) sets the tone for Paul's concerns in 6:1–5. Why would the Galatian Christians be conceited? They had experienced 'so much' through the Spirit (3:4–5), but some evidently thought they were quite something as a result. Paul tells such Christians that they are deceived (v. 3). Life in the Spirit is not a competition (5:26). In addition, the agitators have no doubt also caused divisions among the churches. Paul tackles the situation by stressing the need for gentle restoration where there has been 'transgression' (and, as we have seen, there are 15 'transgressions' to choose from in chapter 5). Moving beyond transgressions, Paul exhorts these conflicted Christian communities to 'bear one another's burdens', for in so doing they 'fulfil the law of Christ' (v. 2). To those who want to follow the law, Paul says that they should look to the law of Christ—that is, 'love your neighbour' (5:14). Getting stuck into community life in love is what this means, as well as working 'for the good of all' while there is time in this age (v. 10).

The postscript in verses 11–18 returns to the key themes of the letter. Paul again refers to the agitators who want to make a 'good showing' in terms of their pro-circumcision campaign (vv. 12–13). To maintain their position in the Jewish community and to avoid persecution from militant Jewish groups, they 'save their own skins by cutting off other people's foreskins' (Wright, p. 82).

The crucifixion of our Lord Jesus Christ is at the heart of Galatians (1:4; 2:19–21; 3:13; 5:11, 24; 6:12, 14). The power of this present age has been crucified and 'I' now belong to the new creation that has come and is coming (vv. 14–15; 3:28; 5:5). We live in-between the ages, however, so we will come into conflict with the defeated powers, especially when we bear the burdens of those whom the world would prefer we left alone. For all who belong to the new creation (v. 16a), Paul honours them as the 'Israel of God' (v. 16b)—God's extended family of faith.

Guidelines

- Do you see any examples of 'gospel plus…' in your particular context? How would you seek to address them? Does Paul provide any helpful clues?
- Are there occasions when the truth of the gospel requires us to oppose others, as Paul opposed Peter? Do we sometimes need to be less 'nice'?
- What markers of Christian identity do we set up today to create second- or third-class Christians? How can we tear down those barriers?
- The opposition between spirit and the flesh is often misunderstood in the church. How might you overcome this misunderstanding in your Christian community?
- Bearing one another's burdens is fulfilling the law of Christ. In what ways might you and your community challenge the powers that prefer the burdens to stay where they are?
- Paul integrates many aspects of theology in Galatians—ethics, pastoral care, doctrine and biblical interpretation. What might you learn from Paul for your own theologising?

FURTHER READING

Charles B. Cousar, *Galatians* (Interpretation), John Knox Press, 1982.

James Dunn, *The Epistle to the Galatians*, Hendrickson, 1993.

Ronald Fung, *The Epistle to the Galatians*, Eerdmans, 1988.

Tom Wright, *Paul for Everyone: Galatians and Thessalonians*, SPCK, 2002.

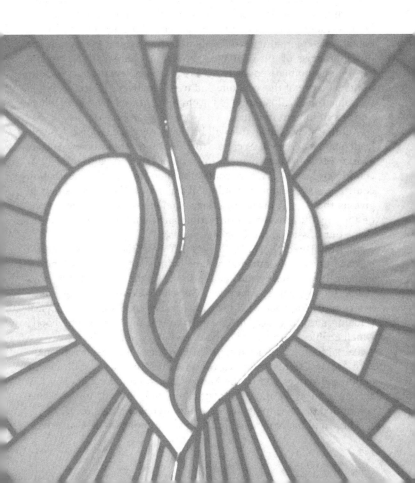

Guidelines forthcoming issue

DAVID SPRIGGS

Our next issue of *Guidelines* takes us through Advent to Christmas and beyond, bringing significant opportunities for us to engage with scripture and prepare ourselves once more for the celebration of 'God with us'.

A new contributor for us will be Pete Wilcox, Dean of Liverpool Cathedral. He tackles one of the most challenging Old Testament books—Judges—with honesty and insight. Not only does this book contain the entertaining stories about Samson, but it focuses on one of the enigmas of our own age—the 'carnal charismatic', as one of my friends summarised the issue. Judges is problematic also because of the violence of those whom God uses to deliver his people, but at the same time it illustrates God's commitment to deliverance, which finds its fulfilment in Christ.

Another new contributor will be David Kerrigan, whose dynamic leadership as General Secretary of the Baptist Missionary Society World Mission has helped to reshape that organisation. For *Guidelines*, he makes a core contribution on the way the incarnation contributes to our understanding of mission. In later issues he will give us the benefit of his experience and engagement as he reflects on the way the cross and resurrection, and then the gift of the Spirit, shape our missional thinking and praxis.

Jill Duff, Director of St Mellitus North West (the St Aidan's Centre) based at Liverpool Cathedral, will be writing for us. Her doctorate is in inorganic chemistry and she is also the mother of two young boys (while Jeremy, her husband, was *Guidelines* Commissioning Editor before me). Together with her parish experience and missiological teaching, she brings deep insight into the 'Spirituality of Motherhood', which enables us to consider the role of Mary in a fresh way.

Paul Moore, best known to BRF readers for his involvement with Messy Church, explores twelve values that are significant for building disciples within the Messy Church context. This is a key challenge in every pioneering situation and, indeed, for everyone committed to developing disciples in our challenging world.

These and many more stimulating sets of notes await you!

Author profile: Bill Goodman

If you have a 'curiosity streak', you will have wondered what our writers are like as flesh-and-blood people. We are now able to let you in on some of their secrets! Our first writer to introduce himself is Bill Goodman, who is contributing to this issue and the next.

I suffer happily from an incurable compulsion to meet with God through wrestling with the Bible and to help other people do the same.

It began in my mid-teens. Having grown up in a family where the divine was way off the radar, I was bemused and delighted to encounter God through a mission at school, led by David Watson. My faith was initially nurtured through summer holiday camps run by Scripture Union, and then at Cambridge University, where I vividly remember Tom Wright giving a series of Bible readings from Luke's Gospel at the Christian Union. The richness and wonder of that portrayal of Jesus became so compelling, I just had to keep coming back for more.

I spent my undergraduate years reading Law, and John Stott. Having completed my degree and developed a burning ambition *not* to be a lawyer, I began to sense a nagging 'mental toothache' (fostered by my vicar, Michael Farrer) about ordination. Ignoring it for as long as I could, I headed off to help develop a theological distance-learning programme in India, at Union Biblical Seminary, for a couple of years. Proofreading study materials helped me feed my own hunger for the Bible, along with that of our students, and my 'toothache' refused to go away.

After theological training at St John's Nottingham came Church of England ordination and a curacy in Burton-upon-Trent. Then I found myself newly married to Sara and serving in parishes in Halifax. With all the delights and demands of ministry, the hunger kept growing. The urge to go deeper led on to a part-time MPhil at the University of Sheffield on 'Wealth and poverty in the book of Revelation', supervised by Loveday Alexander. I completed my studies (slowly!) alongside parish ministry and the birth of our children. Not to forget life's other joys—I love hiking up mountains, sailing in a strong breeze, making and listening to music, keeping up with the news, and exploring new places and possibilities.

When we arrived in Addis Ababa as Crosslinks Mission Partners, I expected to be teaching New Testament. However, Africa teaches you flexibility: the needs of the Seminary and Graduate School where I was working, combined with aspects of the local culture and language, increasingly steered me towards the Old Testament. I really enjoyed those six years helping potential leaders of the fast-growing Ethiopian churches to explore the Bible, and was constantly challenged by the depth of their discipleship. My annual trip with one student to his home village in the countryside helped me understand why his hunger for scripture was so keen, as we preached our way through the weekend to hundreds of spiritually open and attentive people.

Back in the UK and working at a large city-centre church in Leicester, the urge to feed others and feed myself felt as strong as ever. So I went back to the University of Sheffield (full-time) for a PhD called 'Yearning for you', which set the Psalms and Song of Songs in conversation with contemporary rock and worship songs. The topic of conversation was our desire for intimacy with each other and with God: can the two be blurred together or should they be kept distinct? This provided another rich feast of learning from fellow students and scholars, not least my supervisor (Cheryl Exum) and my former tutor at St John's (John Goldingay).

Now I find myself as Continuing Ministerial Development Officer in the Anglican Diocese of Lincoln. There's a fair bit of planning and organising involved, which I don't always relish, but today I'm enjoying preparing a Quiet Day for clergy and lay leaders, reconnecting with the subtlety and richness of Jesus' parables. Some guidance for preachers on the upcoming lectionary readings also needs my attention, and I've been preparing for a seminar with ordinands and trainee readers at the Lincoln School of Theology on the Old Testament Wisdom books. In all this I'm constantly rediscovering the frustrating limits of my own understanding; that compulsion to keep wrestling and learning more along with others remains as incurable as ever!

Recommended reading

KAREN LAISTER and ESTHER TAYLOR

God's Daughters
Loved, held, accepted, enough

HANNAH FYTCHE

pb, 9781841014095, £6.99

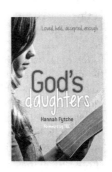

'Do you ever feel like you're not good enough for other people and they will never love or accept you?' Hannah Fytche is only too aware of these feelings and of having to grow up in a culture where there are enormous pressures on young women.

It was her encounter with a passage from 1 Kings 19 that enabled Hannah to see God in a different way and understand that 'God doesn't want us to live craving love and fearing failure when he already loves us and forgives our mistakes'. Hannah explores six issues that young women face today: school, image, friends, family, church and our personal relationship with God.

This book is a must for any Christian teenage girl who is working through those issues of identity and value. Written when Hannah was a teenager, this book provides insights into this critical stage of life and faith development.

Hilda of Whitby
A spirituality for now

RAY SIMPSON

pb, 9781841017280, £7.99

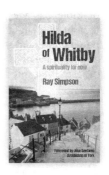

Finding strength in dark times is a challenge we all face, but the power of St Hilda of Whitby—an Anglo-Saxon who lived in a troubled and violent era, among warring pagan tribes—is a testimony to the potential of struggles, and the importance of embracing God during hardship. Published in celebration of the 1400th anniversary of Hilda's birth, this awe-inspiring book is a testimony to the importance of courage, adversity and, above all, faith.

In light of this, one of the most commanding messages in this book is the absolute importance of receptivity. Hilda and her followers trusted the signs they found around them and encouraged the gifts they received, whether they were the songs of Caedmon (a cowherd who was blessed with heavenly music) or the dream Hilda's mother had while she was pregnant, prophesying the role that her daughter would play.

It can be hard to have faith in the insubstantial, in fleeting dreams, but this book testifies to the wonders experienced by surrendering to God's care and accepting him into every part of life.

The Apple of His Eye
Discovering God's loving purpose for each one of us

BRIDGET PLASS

pb, 9781841010885, £7.99

Indeed we are all redeemed by God's love, but *The Apple of his Eye* by Bridget Plass highlights that blessing—the incredible love that he has for each and every one of us. An exploration of Bible passages, this book explores a simple, life-rattling idea: that Jesus delights in us all, that we are more loved than we can understand, and that we are all children of God.

The grace of this love is absolute, and by understanding the words of Jesus we can create lives that praise the glory of God.

Servant Ministry
A portrait of Christ and a pattern for his followers

TONY HORSFALL

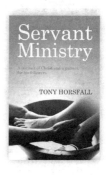

pb, 9780857460882, £7.99

Celebrating the glory of God and stepping up to the challenge of worship can be difficult at times. Being a servant of the Lord, and understanding what servanthood means, can appear complex despite its simplicity. This book by Tony Horsfall refreshingly clarifies the role that believers can have in the work of the church, and the power entrusted to us as children of God.

Servant Ministry offers a guided exposition of the first 'Servant Song' in Isaiah 42:1–9, and illustrates what it really means to be a servant—the highs, the lows, and the grace that the position brings.

Deep Calls to Deep
Spiritual formation in the hard places of life

TONY HORSFALL

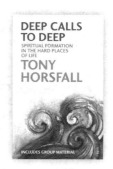

pb, 9781841017310, £7.99

Is there a positive purpose to suffering? The reality of pain, loss and grief is unavoidable, as much a part of life as the beautiful joys. These challenges shape our world, and the struggle often impacts our spiritual growth, harshness and difficulty transforming our spiritual lives. In this book Tony Horsfall postulates that suffering is an inescapable part of the journey to God, and that the seemingly senseless difficulties we face are opportunities for transformation.

Analysing the Psalms of Lament, this book offers a compass to finding God in the hardest of times and being equipped spiritually with the right tools.

80 Creative Prayer Ideas
A resource for church and group use

CLAIRE DANIEL

pb, 9781841016887, £8.99

Prayer can be a source of wonder and joy and enlightenment, but sometimes it can be difficult to carve out a moment dedicated to prayer, to fully embrace the power of what is underway and be entirely in the moment. These 80 prayer ideas are a magnificent resource, creatively bestowing the gift of prayer for the use of churches and groups, so as to magnify the experience and reach out to God in simple but meaningful ways.

This is a book to be celebrated. The act of writing a love letter to God, of praying with water, of using broken pots of clay—these are all linked to higher messages and brought into focus with Bible reflections that enable the thanksgiving, reflection and clarity gifted by prayer. Designed for adults of all ages, these imaginative prayers offer a celebration of God's love, and are made with simple props ranging from stationery to biscuits.

To order a copy of any of these books, please use the order form on pages 149–150. BRF books are also available from your local Christian bookshop or from **www.brfonline.org.uk**.

BRF PUBLICATIONS ORDER FORM

To order our resources online, please visit **www.brfonline.org.uk**

Please send me the following book(s):

		Quantity	Price	Total
417 0	**The Recovery of Hope** Naomi Starkey	_____	£8.99	_____
409 5	**God's Daughters** Hannah Fytche	_____	£6.99	_____
728 0	**Hilda of Whitby** Ray Simpson	_____	£7.99	_____
088 5	**The Apple of His Eye** Bridget Plass	_____	£7.99	_____
088 2	**Servant Ministry** Tony Horsfall	_____	£7.99	_____
731 0	**Deep Calls to Deep** Tony Horsfall	_____	£7.99	_____
688 7	**80 Creative Prayer Ideas** Claire Daniel	_____	£8.99	_____
428 6	**Encountering the Risen Christ** Mark Bradford	_____	£7.99	_____
420 0	**Believe in Miracles** Carmel Thomason	_____	£7.99	_____
427 9	**Postcards from Heaven** Ellie Hart	_____	£7.99	_____
379 1	**Messy Prayer** Jane Leadbetter	_____	£6.99	_____
415 6	**Messy Hospitality** Lucy Moore	_____	£9.99	_____
413 2	**The Gift of Years** (Bible reflections)	_____	£2.50	_____
	Quiet Spaces FREE sample copy	_____	£0.00	_____

Total cost of books £ _____

Donation £ _____

Postage and packing (*see overleaf*) £ _____

TOTAL £ _____

Please complete the payment details below and return with the appropriate payment to: BRF, 15 The Chambers, Vineyard, Abingdon OX14 3FE

Title _____ First name/initials _____ Surname _____

Address _____

_____ Postcode _____

Telephone _____ Email _____

Total enclosed £ _____ (cheques should be made payable to 'BRF')

Please charge my Visa ☐ Mastercard ☐ Maestro ☐ with £ _____

Card no. ☐☐☐☐ ☐☐☐☐ ☐☐☐☐ ☐☐☐☐

Expiry date ☐☐ ☐☐ Security code ☐☐☐

Issue no. (Maestro only) ☐☐☐

Signature (essential if paying by credit card/Maestro) _____

BRF is a Registered Charity (No. 233280)

POSTAGE AND PACKING CHARGES				
Order value	UK	Europe	Economy (Surface)	Standard (Air)
Under £7.00	£1.25	£3.00	£3.50	£5.50
£7.00–£29.99	£2.25	£5.50	£6.50	£10.00
£30.00 & over	FREE	Prices on request		

Transforming Lives and Communities

BRF is a charity that is passionate about making a difference through the Christian faith. We want to see lives and communities transformed through our creative programmes and resources for individuals, churches and schools. We are doing this by resourcing:

- **Christian growth and understanding of the Bible.** Through our Bible reading notes, books, digital resources, Quiet Days and other events, we're resourcing individuals, groups and leaders in churches for their own spiritual journey and for their ministry.

- **Church outreach in the local community.** BRF is the home of three programmes that churches are embracing to great effect as they seek to engage with their local communities: Messy Church, Who Let The Dads Out? and The Gift of Years.

- **Teaching Christianity in primary schools.** Our Barnabas in Schools team is working with primary-aged children and their teachers, enabling them to explore Christianity creatively within the school curriculum.

- **Children's and family ministry.** Through our Barnabas in Churches and Faith in Homes websites and published resources, we're working with churches and families, enabling children under 11, and the adults working with them, to explore Christianity creatively and bring the Bible alive.

Do you share our vision?

Sales of our books and Bible reading notes cover the cost of producing them. However, our other programmes are funded primarily by donations, grants and legacies. If you share our vision, would you help us to transform even more lives and communities? Your prayers and financial support are vital for the work that we do.

- You could support BRF's ministry with a one-off gift or regular donation (using the response form on page 153).
- You could consider making a bequest to BRF in your will (page 152).
- You could encourage your church to support BRF as part of your church's giving to home mission—perhaps focusing on a specific area of our ministry, or a particular member of our Barnabas team.
- Most important of all, you could support BRF with your prayers.

The difference a gift in your Will can make

Gifts left in Wills don't need to be huge to help us make a real difference. Throughout our history, BRF's work has been enabled thanks to the generosity of those who have shared its vision and supported its work by giving both during their lifetime and also through legacy gifts. All have helped BRF in its mission to transform lives and communities through the Christian faith.

One of the fastest growing areas of BRF is Messy Church. Messy Church reaches people of all ages who have often never set foot in a church before, by being 'church' differently. It is being delivered in a variety of contexts in local communities, including care homes, prisons, inner cities, schools and rural areas. Week by week we are seeing new Messy Churches starting up across the UK and around the globe, and across all major Christian denominations. We estimate that over 500,000 people are attending Messy Church each month.

A legacy gift would help fund the growth, development and sustainability of BRF's Messy Church into the future. Would you consider a legacy gift to help us continue to take this work forward in the decades to come?

For further information about making a gift to BRF in your Will or to discuss how a specific bequest could be used to develop our ministry, please contact Sophie Aldred (Head of Fundraising) or Richard Fisher (Chief Executive) by phone on 01865 319700 or by email at fundraising@brf.org.uk.

Whatever you can do or give, we thank you for your support.

BRF MINISTRY APPEAL RESPONSE FORM

I want to help BRF by funding some of its core ministries. Please use my gift for:

☐ where it is needed most ☐ Barnabas Children's Ministry ☐ Messy Church

☐ Who Let The Dads Out? ☐ The Gift of Years

Please complete all relevant sections of this form and print clearly.

Title _____ First name/initials _____ Surname _____

Address _____

_____ Postcode _____

Telephone _____ Email _____

Regular giving

If you would like to give by direct debit, please tick the box below and fill in details:

☐ I would like to make a regular gift of £ _____ per month / quarter / year
(*delete as appropriate*) by direct debit. (*Please also complete the direct debit instruction on page 159.*)

If you would like to give by standing order, please contact Priscilla Kew:
Tel. 01865 319700 | priscilla.kew@brf.org.uk | or write to her at BRF

One-off donation

Please accept my special gift of:

☐ £10 ☐ £50 ☐ £100 (other) £ _____ by

☐ Cheque / Charity Voucher payable to 'BRF' (*delete as appropriate*)

☐ Visa / Mastercard / Charity Card (*delete as appropriate*)

Name on card _____

Card no. ☐☐☐☐ ☐☐☐☐ ☐☐☐☐ ☐☐☐☐

Start date ☐☐☐☐   Expiry date ☐☐☐☐

Security code ☐☐☐

Signature _____ Date _____

☐ I would like to leave a legacy to BRF. Please send me further information.

☐ I would like BRF to claim back tax on this gift. (*If you tick this box, you will need to complete the gift aid declaration overleaf.*)

Please return this completed form to: BRF, 15 The Chambers, Vineyard, Abingdon OX14 3FE

GIFT AID DECLARATION

The Bible Reading Fellowship

Please treat as Gift Aid donations all qualifying gifts
of money made

giftaid it

☐ today,   ☐ in the past four years,   ☐ and in the future.

I confirm I have paid or will pay an amount of Income Tax and/or Capital Gains
Tax for each tax year (6 April to 5 April) that is at least equal to the amount of
tax that all the charities that I donate to will reclaim on my gifts for that tax year.
I understand that other taxes such as VAT or Council Tax do not qualify.
I understand BRF will reclaim 25p of tax on every £1 that I give.

☐ My donation does not qualify for Gift Aid.

Signature _____ Date _____

Notes

1. Please notify BRF if you want to cancel this declaration, change your name
   or home address, or no longer pay sufficient tax on your income and/or
   capital gains.

2. If you pay Income Tax at the higher/additional rate and want to receive the
   additional tax relief due to you, you must include all your Gift Aid donations
   on your Self-Assessment tax return or ask HM Revenue and Customs to adjust
   your tax code.

We like to acknowledge all donations. However, if you do not wish to receive
an acknowledgement, please tick here ☐

GL0216

How to encourage Bible reading in your church

BRF has been helping individuals connect with the Bible for over 90 years. We want to support churches as they seek to encourage church members into regular Bible reading.

Order a Bible reading resources pack

This pack is designed to give your church the tools to publicise our Bible reading notes. It includes:

• Sample Bible reading notes for your congregation to try.

• Publicity resources, including a poster.

• A church magazine feature about Bible reading notes.

The pack is free, but we welcome a £5 donation to cover the cost of postage. If you require a pack to be sent outside the UK or require a specific number of sample Bible reading notes, please contact us for postage costs. More information about what the current pack contains is available on our website.

How to order and find out more

• Visit www.biblereadingnotes.org.uk/for-churches

• Telephone BRF on 01865 319700 between 9.15 am and 5.30 pm

• Write to us at BRF, 15 The Chambers, Vineyard, Abingdon OX14 3FE

Keep informed about our latest initiatives

We are continuing to develop resources to help churches encourage people into regular Bible reading, wherever they are on their journey. Join our email list at www.biblereadingnotes.org.uk/helpingchurches to stay informed about the latest initiatives that your church could benefit from.

Introduce a friend to our notes

We can send information about our notes and current prices for you to pass on. Please contact us.

GUIDELINES INDIVIDUAL SUBSCRIPTION FORM

All our Bible reading notes can be ordered online by visiting
www.biblereadingnotes.org.uk/subscriptions

☐ I would like to take out a subscription:

Title _____ First name/initials _____ Surname _____

Address _____

_____ Postcode _____

Telephone _____ Email _____

Please send **Guidelines** beginning with the September 2016 / January 2017 /
May 2017 issue (*delete as appropriate*):

(*please tick box*)	UK	Europe/Economy	Airmail
Guidelines	☐ £16.35	☐ £24.90	☐ £28.20
Guidelines 3-year subscription	☐ £43.20	N/A	N/A

Please complete the payment details below and return with the appropriate
payment to: BRF, 15 The Chambers, Vineyard, Abingdon OX14 3FE

Total enclosed £ _____ (cheques should be made payable to 'BRF')

Please charge my Visa ☐ Mastercard ☐ Maestro ☐ with £ _____

Card no. ☐☐☐☐ ☐☐☐☐ ☐☐☐☐ ☐☐☐☐

Expiry date ☐☐☐☐ Security code ☐☐☐

Issue no. (Maestro only) ☐☐☐☐

Signature (essential if paying by credit card/Maestro) _____

To set up a direct debit, please also complete the direct debit instruction
on page 159 and return it to BRF with this form.

GL0216

GUIDELINES GIFT SUBSCRIPTION FORM

☐ I would like to give a gift subscription (please provide both names and addresses):

Title _____ First name/initials _____ Surname _____

Address _____

_____ Postcode _____

Telephone _____ Email _____

Gift subscription name _____

Gift subscription address _____

_____ Postcode _____

Gift message (20 words max. or include your own gift card):

_____

_____

Please send Guidelines beginning with the September 2016 / January 2017 / May 2017 issue (*delete as appropriate*):

(*please tick box*)	UK	Europe/Economy	Airmail
Guidelines	☐ £16.35	☐ £24.90	☐ £28.20
Guidelines 3-year subscription	☐ £43.20	N/A	N/A

Please complete the payment details below and return with the appropriate payment to: BRF, 15 The Chambers, Vineyard, Abingdon OX14 3FE

Total enclosed £ _____ (cheques should be made payable to 'BRF')

Please charge my Visa ☐ Mastercard ☐ Maestro ☐ with £ _____

Card no. ☐☐☐☐ ☐☐☐☐ ☐☐☐☐ ☐☐☐☐

Expiry date ☐☐ ☐☐   Security code ☐☐☐

Issue no. (Maestro only) ☐☐☐☐

Signature (essential if paying by credit card/Maestro) _____

To set up a direct debit, please also complete the direct debit instruction on page 159 and return it to BRF with this form.

BRF is a Registered Charity (No. 233280)

DIRECT DEBIT PAYMENT

You can pay for your annual subscription to our Bible reading notes using Direct Debit. You need only give your bank details once, and the payment is made automatically every year until you cancel it. If you would like to pay by Direct Debit, please use the form opposite, entering your BRF account number under 'Reference'.

You are fully covered by the Direct Debit Guarantee:

The Direct Debit Guarantee

· This Guarantee is offered by all banks and building societies that accept instructions to pay Direct Debits.

· If there are any changes to the amount, date or frequency of your Direct Debit, The Bible Reading Fellowship will notify you 10 working days in advance of your account being debited or as otherwise agreed. If you request The Bible Reading Fellowship to collect a payment, confirmation of the amount and date will be given to you at the time of the request.

· If an error is made in the payment of your Direct Debit, by The Bible Reading Fellowship or your bank or building society, you are entitled to a full and immediate refund of the amount paid from your bank or building society.

· If you receive a refund you are not entitled to, you must pay it back when The Bible Reading Fellowship asks you to.

· You can cancel a Direct Debit at any time by simply contacting your bank or building society. Written confirmation may be required. Please also notify us.

The Bible Reading Fellowship

Instruction to your bank or building society to pay by Direct Debit

Please fill in the whole form using a ballpoint pen and return it to:
BRF, 15 The Chambers, Vineyard, Abingdon OX14 3FE

Service User Number: | 5 | 5 | 8 | 2 | 2 | 9 |

Name and full postal address of your bank or building society

To: The Manager	Bank/Building Society
Address	
	Postcode

Name(s) of account holder(s)

Branch sort code

| | | | | | |

Bank/Building Society account number

| | | | | | | | |

Reference

| | | | | | | | |

Instruction to your Bank/Building Society
Please pay The Bible Reading Fellowship Direct Debits from the account detailed in this instruction, subject to the safeguards assured by the Direct Debit Guarantee. I understand that this instruction may remain with The Bible Reading Fellowship and, if so, details will be passed electronically to my bank/building society.

Signature(s)

Banks and Building Societies may not accept Direct Debit instructions for some types of account.

This page is for your notes.